GLOBALIZATION
AND
INEQUALITY

GLOBALIZATION
AND
INEQUALITY

Elhanan Helpman

Harvard University Press

Cambridge, Massachusetts, and London, England   2018

Library of Congress Cataloging-in-Publication Data

Names: Helpman, Elhanan, author.

Title: Globalization and inequality / Elhanan Helpman.

Description: Cambridge, Massachusetts : Harvard University Press, 2018. |
Includes bibliographical references and index.

Identifiers: LCCN 2017060589 | ISBN 9780674984608 (alk. paper)

Subjects: LCSH: Income distribution. | Globalization–Economic aspects. |
Technological innovations–Economic aspects.

Classification: LCC HC79.I5 H454 2018 | DDC 339.2/2–dc23 LC record
available at https://lccn.loc.gov/2017060589

To Ella

Contents

Contents

Preface

Opposition to globalization has become widespread, and concerns about growing inequality have gained prominence. Moreover, although part of the objection to globalization is based on social and political concerns such as cultural autonomy, child labor, or domestic sovereignty, a notable portion is founded on the argument that globalization raises income disparity. The aim of this book is to address this latter argument. Building on an extensive literature, I will review the theoretical mechanisms through which foreign trade and offshoring affect earnings inequality and the evidence on their quantitative effects. Other aspects of globalization, such as international capital flows or migration, will be addressed only in passing.

I hope that experts and nonexperts alike will find this treatise interesting. Although most of the literature on this subject is technical, I have sought to explain the arguments in plain English for the benefit of readers who are not trained in economic discourse. In style, this book is similar to two of my previous books: *The Mystery of Economic Growth* and *Understanding Global Trade*.

My decision to write this book developed over several years. While researching this subject, I became fascinated with the intricacies of the arguments and the innumerable challenges posed to empirical investigations of the contribution of globalization to inequality. Furthermore, although great progress has been made over a quarter century of research on this topic, I became aware that much of the public debate did not use the available evidence and that a satisfactory understanding of trade and inequality was also lacking in the economics profession. A series of lectures to various audiences strengthened my conviction. These include the Frisch Memorial Lecture (World Congress of the Econometric Society, Shanghai, China, 2010), the RIETI International Seminar Distinguished Lecture (Tokyo, Japan, 2011), a keynote address at the Conference on Globalization and Labor Markets (Geneva, Switzerland, 2011), the EJ Lecture (Royal Economic Society Annual Conference, Cambridge, UK, 2012), a keynote address at the Banque de France Conference on Globalization and Labor Market Outcomes (Paris, France, 2013), the Merrick Lecture (University of Virginia, Charlottesville, VA, USA, 2013), the Robert Bradbury Distinguished Lecture on International Economics (University of Florida, Gainesville, FL, USA, 2013), the Kuznets Lecture (Yale University, New Haven, CT, USA, 2014), a keynote address at the International Economics and Financial Society of China Annual Conference (Beijing, China, 2014), a keynote address at the Warsaw International Economic Meeting (Warsaw, Poland, 2014), a keynote address at the 7th FIW-Research Conference on International Economics (Vienna, Austria, 2014), the Jean-Jacques Laffont Lecture (Toulouse School of Economics, Toulouse, France, 2015), and the RCEF2016 Lecture (Rimini Conference in Economics and Finance, Waterloo, Ontario, Canada, 2016).

When the British Academy invited me to deliver the Keynes Lecture in Economics, I decided to use this opportunity to explore the possibility of writing a book on globalization and inequality. That lecture, "Globalisation and Wage Inequality," was given on September 28, 2016, and published in the *Journal of the British Academy* (volume 5 [July 19, 2017]: 125–162, © The British Academy 2017, doi.org/10.5871/jba/005.125). The subject, however, warranted a book. A half-year sabbatical from Harvard University facilitated this project. During this sabbatical, I visited the Berglas School of Economics at Tel Aviv University, CREI at Universitat Pompeu Fabra, the Department of Economics at the London School of Economics, and the Department of Economics at Bocconi University. In each one of these institutions, I wrote part of the manuscript. I am very grateful to my hosts in these institutions for providing excellent conditions for my visits.

Many people helped me to understand the complex interactions between the growing integration of the world economy and its implications for inequality. First and foremost are my coauthors: Gene Grossman, Oleg Itskhoki, Philipp Kircher, Marc Muendler, and Stephen Redding. Second are scholars who were kind enough to comment on my manuscript: Daron Acemoglu, Donald Davis, Gino Gancia, Gene Grossman, Gordon Hanson, Brian Kovak, Eunhee Lee, Marc Melitz, Marc Muendler, Torsten Persson, Assaf Razin, Stephen Redding, Elisa Rubbo, and Efraim Sadka. I am grateful to all of them. Third are my colleagues at the Canadian Institute for Advanced Research (CIFAR), whose feedback on my work has been extremely helpful. And finally, my assistant, Jane Trahan, who devoted all of her energies to improving the narrative of this manuscript, as she did with my previous two books. Jane has been a great resource for twenty years, and I am most grateful for all of her services.

GLOBALIZATION

AND

INEQUALITY

Introduction

INTERNATIONAL COMMERCE has a long history in the evolution of the world's economy, dating back to biblical times more than three thousand years ago and extending through the Roman Empire, the Dark Ages, the Middle Ages, and the post–Industrial Revolution era (see McCormick 2001, Findlay and O'Rourke 2007, and Helpman 2011, chap. 1). Despite this long history, imports plus exports as a share of the value of output were very small until the beginning of the nineteenth century. As I explain in Chapter 1, the value of the world's imports plus exports amounted to 2 percent of the value of the world's output around 1820; and it kept rising until World War I. This was the first documented wave of globalization. The second wave started after World War II and has not yet abated.

The drivers of globalization changed over time. According to Baldwin (2016), in the first phase, referred to as the "first unbundling," declining costs of shipping drove the process. In the second phase, which Baldwin called the "second unbundling," the costs of situating parts of the manufacturing process in different geographical areas declined; and this encouraged the fragmentation of the production process across international borders. As a result, global supply chains emerged. The third phase, or the "third unbundling," still in its infancy, is dominated by declining costs of face-to-face interaction between individuals in different parts of the world. Although the first and second phases of globalization were characterized by a rapid expansion of *merchandise* trade, the second phase was also marked by a rapid expansion of trade in *services*, especially business services.

Globalization has been blamed for rising inequality in both rich and poor countries, and antiglobalization demonstrations have become a common feature at international meetings, be they of the World Bank, the International Monetary Fund, the G7 countries, or the G20 countries. A heated debate about the merits and faults of globalization has arisen in recent decades. Yet the views of many protagonists in this debate are not based on evidence. Moreover, many political activists espouse a caricature of the economic arguments in favor of free trade.

Indeed, many professional economists, such as Bhagwati (1988, 2002), do emphasize the aggregate gains from trade as a central tenet in the design of international institutions whose goal is to benefit all. But at the same time, economists understand that the *aggregate* benefits may not be equitably distributed among the world's citizens (see Helpman 2011, chap. 3). Scholars have studied the costs and benefits of globalization, and the policies for promoting or taming it, in order to form an educated viewpoint. These types of studies require extensive knowledge of economics, including theoretical and empirical methods. Forming a reliable opinion on these matters is really not feasible without such research. Once the findings of these studies are comprehended, however, it is possible to draw dependable conclusions about desirable policies and outcomes. Of course, not everyone is likely to draw the same conclusions, mostly because different individuals may place distinct weights on various costs and benefits.

To help form an evidence-based opinion on this matter, this book examines the theoretical and empirical literature on the relationship between globalization and the inequality of earnings. Although I will touch on foreign direct investment and international migration, too, the focus will be on international trade.

In 1870, foreign capital amounted to less than 10 percent of the combined gross domestic product (GDP) of developing countries; and this share peaked at 32.4 percent in 1914, on the eve of World War I. This stock of foreign assets declined afterward and bottomed out at less than 5 percent of GDP in 1950 (see figure 1.1 in Chandy and Seidel 2016). After World War II, as part of the second wave of globalization, international capital flows greatly expanded. Early on, following the adoption of the Bretton Woods international monetary system, most countries embraced fixed exchange rates and controls on international capital mobility. But the fixed exchange rate system collapsed in 1971; and restrictions on capital flows were gradually removed, first in rich countries, then in the developing world. As a result, cross-border holdings of financial and nonfinancial assets rapidly expanded, exceeding 30 percent of GDP in the developing world after the rebound from the financial crisis of 2008. How did capital account liberalization reforms affect inequality? Available studies report correlations, with no hard evidence about causes. Both Jaumotte, Lall, and Papageorgiou (2008) and Furceri and Loungani (2015) reported that across countries, capital account liberalization was positively correlated with increases in the Gini coefficient of the distribution of income (that is, with increased inequality). Yet the mechanisms that drove this correlation have not been deciphered.

International migration has been a feature of the international landscape for many years, too. According to Ferrie and Hatton (2015, figure 2.1), intercontinental emigration from Europe amounted to more than 200,000 individuals per annum in the mid-nineteenth century and started to rise significantly toward the end of that century, reaching a peak of more than 1.4 million in the early twentieth century. The flow of immigrants declined to less than 200,000 in the late 1930s but started to grow again in the 1960s. The world's stock of foreign-born residents was 2.3 percent of the world's population in

1965 (amounting to 75.2 million people), and it increased to 3.1 percent in 2010 (amounting to 213.9 million) (see their table 2.2).

Despite these fluctuations, multiple studies found very limited effects of migration on wages. In his Richard T. Ely Lecture to the American Economic Association, Card (2009) evaluated the impact of immigrants on wages, using variation across US cities. From studying these data, he concluded that overall immigration had little effect on wage inequality among native-born individuals in the United States. Further, accounting for wages of immigrants, Card found that "immigrants can explain about 5 percent of the rise in overall wage inequality between 1980 and 2000" (p. 3), a small fraction indeed. Blau and Kahn (2015), who reviewed a large number of studies of multiple countries, reached a similar conclusion. And the same conclusion was echoed in the review of the literature by Peri (2016). In short, although I do not examine in detail the impact of immigration on inequality, there appears to be broad agreement among experts that it is small.

The rest of this book describes the prolonged effort by economists to unearth the relationship between the inequality of earnings and globalization in the form of foreign trade and offshoring. This effort has spanned a quarter century, building on the insights of some of the most distinguished scholars of foreign trade and labor economics. After providing a brief historical background on the evolution of inequality within countries and across the globe, I describe how the professional thinking on the subject has advanced. This progression has been fascinating.

The initial attempts to interpret the rise of inequality in the 1980s using the traditional theory of international trade are described in Part I. These efforts led to the conclusion that trade and offshoring contributed little to the widening gap in wages between highly skilled individuals and workers with low skills. But the theory that was used for this purpose proved to be inadequate, because it did not sit comfortably with various pieces of the evidence. In response, new theoretical frameworks were brought to bear on this issue. The new models identified mechanisms of influence that were not present in the traditional theory, that were more suitable for addressing the new realities, and that could be studied with richer data sets and new empirical methods that became available over time. This broadening of the canvas is described in Part II.

In both parts of this book, the interplay between theoretical and empirical analysis plays a central role. Some of the theoretical developments were a response to evidence, while some of the evidence was discovered with the aid of new theoretical insights. As is common in economics, every theoretical model was designed to focus on a *particular* link between international trade and the structure of earnings, which means that other links were disregarded (see Rodrik 2015 for a discussion of this methodology). The advantage of this approach is that it clearly states the ways in which the modelled link is thought to shape inequality, and it informs researchers about the appropriate data and empirical analysis that should be used to test or quantify this relationship. It is then possible to go to the data and assess the importance of this link. Much of the work discussed in this book follows this path. An example is the work of Kovak (see Chapter 7), which links changes in product prices due to a tariff reform to changes in regional wages and wage disparity across Brazil.

Yet there are disadvantages to this research strategy, too. By attempting to study every channel of influence in isolation, no impact is attributed to the *interactions* between competing or complementary mechanisms. This is unfortunate, because such interactions can be important. As an example, consider the discussion (in Chapter 4) about the role of trade or technology in forming inequality. There, trade and technology were studied as competing influences. But in some of these studies, no account was taken of the possible effects of technology on trade, and none of them considered the possible effect of trade on technology. Or take the studies (in Chapter 9) in which trade and offshoring guided investment in research and development and thereby had an effect on the nature of technological change. In this world, trade has a direct impact on wages and an indirect effect through technical change. When this is the case, estimating the impact of trade or offshoring on inequality in isolation from its impact on technical change may bias the estimates upward or downward. In short, the theory that guides empirical studies influences the estimates in important ways, and one needs to be aware of this fact when interpreting the evidence.

Sometimes, scholars study data sets with no explicit theory in mind. These types of studies look for patterns in the data and are especially useful when new data sets become available. From these studies, stylized facts (simple statements of the observed patterns) emerge. Predictions of the currently held theoretical models can then be examined to see whether they are consistent with these stylized facts. If they are not, attempts can be made to modify the models to make them more consistent with the evidence. This consistency is only qualitative, however, which does not guarantee that estimating the new theoretical model with these data will yield a satisfactory fit. When the fit is good, it builds confidence in the theoretical model. When it is not so good, it is necessary to find other modifications of the theory to improve the fit. Chapter 10, about residual inequality, illustrates this approach.

Structural empirical models, which often embody several channels that link globalization to inequality, provide an alternative to direct estimation of the links of interest. These models can be used for counterfactual analysis, which is often not possible with reduced form estimates of specific linkages. Thus, for example, one can use them to answer the following question: What would be the structure of earnings if countries did not trade with each other? In a rich enough structural model, the answer to this question embodies the interaction of several channels through which globalization affects inequality (see

Chapter 6 for illustrations). The disadvantage of these types of models is that their quantification relies on highly specific building blocks and values of parameters that were estimated with other data sets.

As the reader can see, there are many ways to study the impact of globalization on inequality. In the following chapters, I discuss studies that used different methods of analysis and explain the application of these methods to various empirical experiences. The latter include trade liberalization in the form of free trade agreements, such as NAFTA and MERCOSUR, or trade expansion through unilateral policies such as China's or Mexico's. Although, by choice, I do not review every study in the huge literature on globalization and inequality, I believe that my selections provide a balanced view of this research. The overwhelming conclusion from these studies, which cover data sets from multiple countries and a variety of research designs, is that globalization has increased the dispersion of earnings in many (but not all) cases, although not by much compared to the actual rise in inequality. In other words, the surprising result is that rising inequality in recent decades has been predominantly driven by forces other than globalization.

It is prudent to think about this as a tentative conclusion, however. As the reader of this book will recognize, the relationship between globalization and inequality is complex and hard to measure. Despite the many advances in this research, dark corners remain. The Conclusion, which summarizes the findings, also discusses some pertinent issues that remain unresolved.

Some readers may find these conclusions unsatisfactory, because they would prefer definitive replies. To them I say that these are the best answers available, and the journey to reach them has been fascinating in its own right. By reading this book, one will better understand the mechanisms that link globalization to inequality and better appreciate the evidence on their quantitative effects. It will help these readers to form an educated opinion on one of the biggest concerns of our time.

1

Historical Background

INCOME INEQUALITY is driven by many factors. In countries that engage in international trade, these factors include internal features—such as the characteristics of the workforce, labor market institutions, and government policies—as well as features of each country's trade partners. Inequality levels of trading countries are interdependent: A country's attributes affect not only the earnings of its own residents but also the earnings of its trade partners' residents. This effect is transmitted through multiple channels. We therefore need to understand how globalization works its way into individual earnings in order to understand how it shapes income inequality.

Historically, income levels evolved in tandem with globalization. According to Maddison (2001), the growth of income per capita was dismal until the beginning of the nineteenth century. Around 1820, growth picked up and continued to accelerate until World War I. Between World War I and World War II, growth slowed, although it remained high by historical standards. Subsequent to World War II, the world economy experienced a golden age of economic growth, with an average growth rate of income per capita close to 3 percent per annum between 1950 and 1973. Growth sagged again in the aftermath

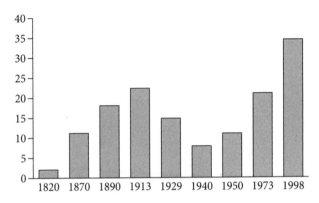

Figure 1.1 World imports plus exports as a percent of world GDP. *Data source:* updated from Estevadeordal, Frantz, and Taylor (2003).

of the oil crisis of 1973; although, like before, it remained high by historical standards (see Helpman 2004, figure 1.5).

Globalization in the form of trade expansion also picked up at the beginning of the nineteenth century. As Figure 1.1 shows, the volume of world trade, as measured by imports plus exports, was 2 percent of world income in 1820; in 1998, it was close to 35 percent.[1] In between, the volume of world trade fluctuated, increasing from the beginning of the nineteenth century until World War I and declining between the two world wars. After World War II, the ratio of trade to income kept rising. Figure 1.1 shows two clear waves of globalization: one before World War I, the other after World War II. Figure 1.2 shows that world trade relative to GDP kept rising in later years, exceeding 60 percent on the eve of the financial crisis of 2008.[2] The financial crisis caused a temporary collapse of international trade.

Inequality of personal income among the world's citizens rose from 1820 to the 1950s and then remained relatively constant, with some fluctuations, until 2000.[3] This pattern is depicted in Figure 1.3 by the height of the bars, each bar representing the Theil coefficient of inequality for a particular year.[4] Figure 1.3 also presents the decom-

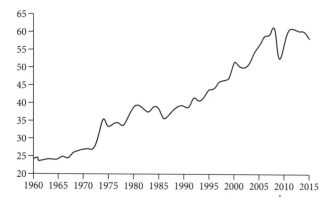

Figure 1.2 World imports and exports of goods and services as a percent of world GDP. *Data source:* World Bank, https://data.worldbank.org/indicator/TG.VAL.TOTL.GD.ZS, accessed on October 16, 2017.

position of this inequality measure into inequality within countries (the lower bars) and inequality between countries (the upper bars). In the latter case, the coefficient is calculated under the supposition that within each country all individuals share the same income, equal to the country's income per capita. As is evident from Figure 1.3, within-country inequality changed little over time, and the rise in overall inequality between 1820 and 1950 was driven primarily by rising inequality between countries. In other words, the income-per-capita gap widened between rich and poor countries as richer countries grew richer over time at a faster pace than did poorer countries, thereby contributing to rising global inequality. Another way to see this phenomenon is by observing that the *share* of between-country inequality in total inequality increased from 38 percent in 1820 to 72 percent in 1950, and this share changed little thereafter.

Although the contribution of within-country inequality to global inequality has been constant from the middle of the twentieth century until 2000, this stability masks substantial differences in inequality trends over time between different countries. Of particular

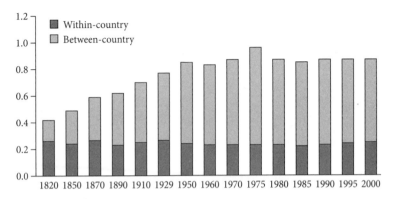

Figure 1.3 The Theil coefficient of the world's distribution of personal income: decomposition into inequality within and between countries. *Data source:* van Zanden, Baten, Foldvari, and van Leeuwen (2014), using the 2005 benchmark.

interest is the fact that in a large number of Organisation for Economic Co-operation and Development (OECD) countries, inequality has substantially increased during this period. This trend has been pronounced in the United States, as can be seen in Figure 1.4, which plots the Gini coefficient of the distribution of men's earnings. According to this measure, inequality declined from 1939 until about 1950 but has been rising ever since, initially at a slow pace and faster since the 1970s.[5] Between the mid-1980s and 2013, income inequality declined slightly in Greece and Turkey and changed very little in Belgium, the Netherlands, and France. In all other OECD countries, income inequality increased substantially, especially so in Finland, Sweden, New Zealand, the United States, and Mexico (see OECD 2015, figure 1.3).

Figure 1.5 depicts the evolution of the Gini coefficient in six OECD countries—the United States, Canada, the Netherlands, Finland, Sweden, and Denmark—from 1989 to 2007. Although in 1989 the United States was the most unequal among these countries and

Figure 1.4 The Gini coefficient of the US distribution of men's earnings. *Data source:* Kopczuk, Saez, and Song (2010). http://www.columbia.edu/~wk2110/uncovering/Figure3-GinicoefficientAnnualEarningsvs5-YearEarnings.csv, accessed on March 17, 2014.

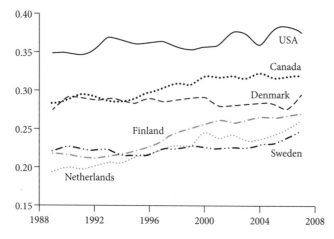

Figure 1.5 The evolution of the Gini coefficient of market income in six OECD countries, 1989–2007. *Data source:* OECD Income distribution and poverty database: http://dx.doi.org/10.1787/888932535204, accessed on December 13, 2016.

Sweden was the least unequal, inequality increased in each of them. Evidently, rising inequality has been a widespread phenomenon.

Although uneven growth between rich and poor countries was responsible for the rising global inequality of individual incomes from the early part of the nineteenth century to the middle of the twentieth century, the more recent rapid growth of less-developed countries has reduced the share of people living in extreme poverty in the developing world. Figure 1.6 shows this decline from 1981 to 2008. In 1981, more than half the population of less-developed countries lived in extreme poverty—defined as income of less than 1.25 purchasing power parity (PPP) adjusted 2005 dollars per day. This share dropped to less than a quarter in 2008. Put another way, although in 1981 close to two billion people lived in extreme poverty, slightly fewer than 1.3 billion people lived in extreme poverty in 2008. Evidently, extreme poverty declined dramatically during this period, most likely aided by globalization.[6] To understand how trade affects between-country inequality, we need to understand how trade affects growth in poor countries relative to that in rich countries. Unfortunately, there is a paucity of research on this topic.

Poverty in low-income countries is measured with an absolute yardstick of 1.25 dollars per day, independently of income per capita. People below this threshold are considered to live in *extreme* poverty, a state of meager survival, and this fraction of people makes up the poverty index. In rich countries, this form of poverty is almost nonexistent; and the prevalent view is that poverty needs to be measured in *relative* terms so that the richer the country, the larger should be the poverty threshold. A common poverty index in these countries is the fraction of people living on less than half the country's median income. This measure is, however, highly correlated with indexes of overall inequality, such as the Gini coefficient (see, for example, figure 8.7 in Morelli, Smeeding, and Thompson 2015), despite the fact that theoretically it does not have to be. This suggests that important

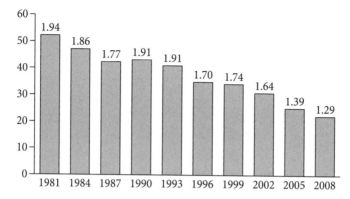

Figure 1.6 Percent and number (in billions on top of the bars) of developing-world people with 2005 Purchasing Power Parity–adjusted income of less than 1.25 dollars per day. *Data source:* Anand and Segal (2015, table 11.8).

properties of income distribution are similar across countries with different levels of income per capita. For this reason, variation across rich countries in overall inequality is similar to the variation in rich countries' poverty rates.

Aversion to within-country inequality is widespread (unfortunately, less so to global inequality). As a result, governments use taxes and transfers to redistribute income. For this reason, disposable income is more equally distributed than is market income. This is illustrated in Figure 1.7 for a sample of twenty-one countries in 2010, where the dark bars represent Gini coefficients of income prior to taxes and transfers, while the light bars represent Gini coefficients of disposable income. In all of these countries, inequality of disposable income is smaller than inequality of market income.

Figure 1.7 also shows that the extent of redistribution varies across countries. As a case in point, compare Greece to Ireland. The latter country has the highest inequality of market income in this sample, while Greece (which also is a high-inequality country) has a significantly lower Gini coefficient of pretax and transfer income;

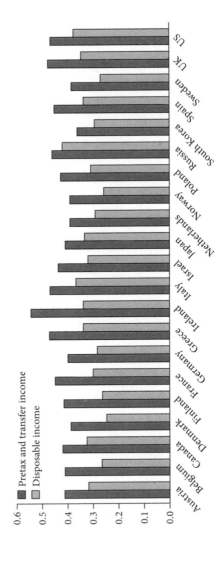

Figure 1.7 Gini coefficients of pretax and transfer and disposable income levels, 2010. *Data source:* Morelli, Smeeding, and Thompson (2015, table 8.4).

nevertheless, both countries end up with similar Gini coefficients of *disposable* income, which implies that Ireland engaged in considerably more redistribution than did Greece.

As another example, compare Canada and Finland, which have similar levels of inequality of market incomes. Yet Finland engages in more redistribution, and it has a significantly lower Gini coefficient of disposable income. Finally, note that Russia has one of the highest inequality levels of pretax and transfer incomes, although not as high as Ireland, Greece, the United Kingdom, or the United States. Nevertheless, Russia has the highest Gini of disposable income, and the gap between this Gini and Russia's Gini of market income is small. Evidently, the Russian tax and transfer system has a small equalizing effect on disposable income.

We have seen that US income inequality, as measured by the Gini coefficient, evolved during the twentieth century in a U-shaped fashion; that is, it declined initially and rose sharply later in the century. Other US measures of inequality also follow a U-shaped pattern. Figure 1.8 depicts this pattern for the income shares of the top 1 percent and top 0.1 percent of US income earners. According to

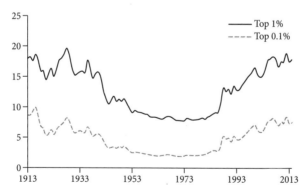

Figure 1.8 Income shares of the richest 1% and 0.1% of US income earners: 1913–2014. *Data source:* The World Wealth and Income Database (WID), http://www.wid.world, accessed on December 9, 2015.

these data, in 1913 individuals in the top 1 percent of the income distribution received 18 percent of US income; their share dropped to a
low of 8 percent in the mid-1970s, and it climbed back to 18 percent
at the end of the sample period. Atkinson, Piketty, and Saez (2011)
report that from 1976 through 2007, these richest individuals captured 58 percent of the growth in US income, including 45 percent
of income growth during the Clinton expansion of 1993 through
2000 and 65 percent of income growth during the Bush expansion
of 2002 through 2007. They also show (see their figure 3) that from
the mid-1970s until 2007, the rapid rise in inequality at the very top
(the richest 0.1 percent of individuals) was caused by rising labor income (wages and salaries plus bonuses, exercised stock options, and
pensions), with capital income playing a secondary role. These data
suggest that although wealth inequality has increased, capital income
did not play a big role in the rise of income inequality until the Great
Recession. According to Piketty, Saez, and Zucman (2018), however,
the contribution of capital to income inequality has increased more
recently, and it may play an even bigger role in the future.[7]

The long-term trends described in this chapter concerning economic growth, globalization, and income inequality may have been
intertwined. Recent concerns about these issues are more narrowly
focused, however, on individual countries. This is because even
though the contribution of within-country inequality to total inequality of the world distribution of personal income was stable
between 1981 and 2000, big changes occurred in individual countries during that period and afterward. Earnings gaps between skilled
and unskilled workers, which played a large role in rising income
inequality from the late 1970s to the early 1990s, increased both in
OECD countries and in less-developed countries. The latter include
countries such as China and India that managed to significantly close
their income gap with the rich economies. At the same time, extreme
poverty declined worldwide, despite population growth that was concentrated in low-income countries.

When worrying about increasing inequality within countries, it is worth remembering that both the number and the fraction of extremely poor people is now much lower than it was thirty years ago; and it is hard to imagine how this could have happened in the absence of globalization. The sources of the rise in within-country inequality have been hotly debated, and a great deal of research has attempted to unearth them. The findings of this research are discussed in the following chapters.

PART I

THE TRADITIONAL APPROACH

OUR UNDERSTANDING of the impact of globalization on inequality has evolved over time. Most of the initial research that examined this relationship relied on what is known as the factor proportions theory of international trade, which was originally developed by Heckscher (1919) and Ohlin (1924, 1933).

In Chapter 2, I describe the dramatic rise in the wage gap between college graduates and high school graduates and elements of the Heckscher-Ohlin theory that were used to explain it. This theory focuses on a small number of aggregates and thus was thought appropriate for considering the distribution of income between skilled and unskilled workers.

As it happened, scholars who engaged in this research concluded that the Heckscher-Ohlin theory was inadequate for explaining these data. The reasons for this conclusion are explained in Chapter 3.

Changes in technology were then proposed as an alternative explanation for the rise in wage inequality in countries at different levels of development. These studies are reviewed and evaluated in Chapter 4.

Next, in Chapter 5, I discuss the extent to which the offshoring of economic activities from rich to poor countries might have increased inequality.

All the theoretical possibilities and the evidence bearing on them covered in Part I of this book are based on the traditional approach to foreign trade. Newly discovered channels that link globalization to inequality are examined in Part II.

2

The Rise of the College Wage Premium

ACCORDING TO the data used to construct Figure 1.8, in 1913 the top 1 percent of US income earners received 18 percent of US income; and this share declined to 8 percent by the mid-1970s. Afterward, the share of the top 1 percent of US income earners climbed to 13 percent in 1990 and to 18 percent in 2008. This U-shaped form of the share of top earners was not unique to the United States (see Atkinson, Piketty, and Saez 2011). In Canada and the United Kingdom, inequality evolved along similar lines.[1] Moreover, inequality has been rising in many countries since the late 1970s, including in the English-speaking countries (the United States, United Kingdom, Canada, Ireland, Australia, and New Zealand), in the Nordic countries (Sweden, Finland, and Norway), and in poorer countries such as India and China.

An important source of the rise in inequality has been growing labor income disparity (see Katz and Autor 1999). Table 2.1 shows changes in the ratio of wages of the 90th percentile earners to the 10th percentile earners in ten OECD countries.[2] In Australia, for example, this ratio was 2.75 in 1979 and increased to 2.94 in 1994. In other words, in 1979 the average Australian wage earner in the 90th percentile earned two-and-three-quarters times more than did the

Table 2.1 Ratio of Wages of the 90th to the 10th Percentile of Male Earners

	Australia	Canada	Finland	France	Italy	Japan	Norway	Sweden	UK	USA
1979	2.75	3.46	2.44	3.39	2.29	2.59	2.05	2.12	2.46	3.19
1994	2.94	3.78	2.53	3.42	2.64	2.77	1.97	2.20	3.22	4.26

Source: Katz and Autor (1999, table 10).

average wage earner in the 10th percentile and close to three times as much in 1994. According to this measure, in 1979 Canada had the highest inequality, France had the second-highest inequality, and the United States had the third-highest inequality. Further, wage inequality increased substantially in the next fifteen years in Canada and the United States, with the United States becoming the most unequal country in 1994. Norway was the least unequal country in 1979, and its inequality slightly declined in the subsequent fifteen years. In all of the other countries in this sample, inequality increased, although the rise in France was minuscule.

Katz and Murphy (1992) studied the change in the number of college graduates relative to high school graduates in the US economy and the corresponding evolution of the relative wages of these two groups of workers. They found that despite the continuous rise in the number of college graduates relative to high school graduates, the college wage premium—which expresses in percentage terms how much more a college graduate earns than a high school graduate—rose sharply in the 1980s. Autor (2014) showed that the relative supply of college graduates, measured by the share of their hours in the aggregate number of hours worked by the adult population, increased continuously from 1963 to 2012. At the same time, the college wage premium followed a humped shape between 1963 and 1979 and sharply increased thereafter, as can be seen in Figure 2.1.[3] The college wage premium was 48 percent in 1979; by 2012, it had doubled to

Figure 2.1 The evolution of the US college wage premium, which measures in percentage terms how much more a college graduate earns than a high school graduate. *Data source:* Autor (2014).

96 percent. In 1987, the last year in the Katz and Murphy sample, the college wage premium was 63 percent.

Katz and Murphy examined the impact of demand and supply factors on the wages of college graduates relative to high school graduates, the idea being that an increase in the relative supply of college graduates should reduce the college wage premium, while an increase in the relative demand should increase it. Among the demand factors, they included international trade and technological change. They concluded that an increase in relative demand dominated the downward pressure from supply to raise the relative wages of college graduates in the US economy. In particular, they noted that while the increased demand for skilled relative to unskilled workers could theoretically be accounted for by shifts in the industrial and occupational composition of employment toward more skill-intensive sectors, in practice the rise in the relative demand for skilled workers reflected primarily an increase in demand *within* rather than *between* sectors (more on this below).

Based on these findings, Katz and Murphy concluded that a particular form of technological change, known as skill-biased technical change, was the principal force behind the rise of the college wage premium; and this conclusion reverberated through many later studies (see Chapter 4 for more details on technology versus trade in shaping the evolution of wages). Factors such as the decline of unionization, the falling value of the minimum wage, and the deregulation of labor and product markets appeared to play a secondary role in the rise of the college wage premium.[4] In the United States, for example, the debate concerning the impact of the minimum wage on inequality led to a nuanced conclusion. Card and DiNardo (2002) argued that the decline in the real value of the minimum wage during the 1980s played a dominant role in the rise of wage inequality. On the other side, Autor, Katz, and Kearney (2008) showed that the minimum wage had an impact on inequality only at the lower end of the wage distribution but not at the upper end, where inequality increased the most. In a more recent analysis, Autor, Manning, and Smith (2016) found that the decline in the real minimum wage explains 30 percent to 40 percent of the rise in wage inequality at the lower tail of the wage distribution in the 1980s (the 50/10 percentile ratio). But they could not reject the hypothesis that the spillovers of wages from the minimum to higher percentiles was due to measurement errors.[5]

Attempts to disentangle the contribution of international trade from the contribution of technology to the rise of the college wage premium came out in favor of technology; that is, that the contribution of technology was more significant. To understand this conclusion, it is necessary to comprehend the forces of globalization that affect wages and to estimate their size. To this end, we conclude Chapter 2 with a discussion of the underlying trade theory, and we review in Chapter 3 the first wave of empirical studies that quantified these effects.

PREMISES OF TRADE THEORY

As a first pass, scholars attempted to interpret the rise of the college wage premium in rich countries as a response to an increase in the relative price of skill-intensive products (that is, products that use a high ratio of skilled relative to unskilled workers in production), caused by international trade. For this purpose, they used the factor proportions trade theory that was originally developed by Eli Heckscher and Bertil Ohlin (see Heckscher 1919; Ohlin 1933). According to this theory, a country that has more skilled relative to unskilled workers produces relatively more high-skill–intensive products. As a result, the country exports high-skill–intensive products, such as computers, and imports low-skill–intensive products, such as footwear (assuming that manufacturers use more high-skilled workers relative to low-skilled workers in the production of computers than in the production of footwear for a given structure of wages).[6] When trade is not impeded by tariffs or transport costs, relative prices are the same in a rich country that has a relatively large endowment of highly skilled workers as in a poor country that has a relatively large endowment of unskilled workers. Under these circumstances, the rich country exports high-skill–intensive products (computers), and the poor country exports low-skill–intensive products (footwear), if both countries have the same expenditure shares when faced with similar prices (preferences are homothetic). This is a key insight from the factor proportions trade theory.

If instead of having free trade, the poor country imposes an import tariff, its domestic relative price of high-skill–intensive products is higher than in the rich country. Then trade liberalization in the poor country would shift down the relative price of computers in that country, thereby reducing the supply of computers relative to footwear in the world economy. As a result of this change in supplies, the relative price of computers would increase in world markets.

Indeed, a group of less-developed countries expanded their participation in foreign trade by reducing barriers to trade and by joining the World Trade Organization (WTO).[7] Compared to rich countries, they specialized in low-skill–intensive products. As a result, their integration into the world's trading system reduced the relative price of low-skill–intensive products; and this change in the terms of trade led to a reallocation of production from low-skill–intensive to high-skill–intensive products in the rich countries. The question is, how did these changes affect the college wage premium?

Wolfgang Stolper and Paul Samuelson provided an answer to this question in a famous article that laid out the Stolper-Samuelson theorem (see Stolper and Samuelson 1941). The theorem states that an increase in the relative price of high-skill–intensive products raises the real wage of skilled workers and reduces the real wage of unskilled workers.[8] Under these circumstances, the college wage premium increases. These wage outcomes do not depend on the sources of the price movements; they can result from a country's change in trade policy, such as enhanced import protection or trade liberalization, or from changes that occur in other countries that trade on international markets. The key is a decline in the relative price of low-skill–intensive products.

In theory, the Stolper-Samuelson mechanism can explain the rise in the college wage premium in rich countries via an increase in the relative price of high-skill–intensive products. The question addressed in Chapter 3 is whether the estimated changes in relative prices and the elasticity of relative wages with respect to relative prices are large enough to explain the data.[9]

This argument has a flip side. For less-developed countries to sell more low-skill–intensive products on world markets after trade liberalization, the relative price of these goods has to rise in their domestic markets, which requires this relative price to be initially lower in less-developed countries than in rich countries. Fortunately for the theory, this type of difference in relative prices is congruent with the presence of import protection in the poorer economies. The logic of the Stolper-Samuelson theorem then implies that following trade liberalization, the college wage premium should decline in these countries, which implies in turn that the skill premium should change in opposite directions in the rich and the poor countries.

Additional implications of this theory concern relative factor use. A higher college wage premium in rich countries induces manufacturers to economize on skilled workers. By the same logic, a lower college wage premium in poor countries induces their manufacturers to economize on low-skilled workers. For this reason, the ratio of high- to low-skilled employees should decline in every sector in rich countries and increase in poor countries. Evidently, once we subscribe to the Stolper-Samuelson mechanism, we also buy into certain subsidiary implications. The empirical validity of these subsidiary implications provides a test of the extent to which this mechanism is suitable for explaining the data (see below).[10]

3

Early Studies

THE FIRST ATTEMPTS at empirically evaluating the role of foreign trade in raising the college wage premium relied on the factor proportions trade theory. In the simplest version of this theory, discussed in Chapter 2, changes in relative prices induce changes in relative factor rewards: An increase in the relative price of high-skill–intensive products raises the real wage of highly skilled workers and reduces the real wage of the unskilled. Therefore, the impact of trade on the college wage premium can be evaluated by estimating two quantities: the impact of trade on relative prices, and the elasticity of relative wages with respect to relative prices. Although this suggests a simple path for quantifying the impact of trade on the college wage premium, producing reliable estimates with this method was difficult due to data limitations (see the discussion in Chapter 4). Given these impediments, early studies proceeded along different routes.

Katz and Murphy (1992) used factor content analysis to compute shifts in labor demand induced by US imports and exports. Their analysis consisted of calculating the services of various factors of production embodied in the country's exports and imports.[1] Adding the net amounts of these services (from imports minus exports) to the country's factor endowment reflects a *notional* country with the same characteristics as the original country except for its factor endowment.[2] The autarky equilibrium, that is, the economic self-sufficient equilibrium of the notional country, is then the same as the trade equilibrium of the original country in terms of prices, factor rewards, and consumption levels. Further, the notional country's output levels in sectors that comprise the original country's exportables equal the original country's output levels minus exports; and the notional country's output levels in sectors that comprise the original country's importables equal the original country's output levels plus imports. In the absence of trade, the original country would be in autarky with its actual factor endowment. Therefore, the gap between the notional country's factor endowment and the original country's factor endowment, which equals the factor content of trade, represents the implicit addition of factor services made available by foreign trade.[3] This gap provides a measure of the pressure that international trade exerts on factor rewards.

An increase in supply depresses a factor's reward, while a reduction in supply raises its reward. If the factor content of trade is small, the gap in factor endowments between the notional country and the actual country is small; and therefore the pressure of trade on factor prices is small. If the factor content of trade is large, the pressure of foreign trade on factor rewards is large. Unfortunately, factor content estimates provide only a partial view of the pressure on factor prices. Converting factor content into changes in factor prices requires estimates of additional features of the economy, such as its sectoral factor intensities and the ease with which low-skilled workers can replace high-skilled workers in production. The latter is gauged by the elasticity of substitution between these workers.

Katz and Murphy (1992) found that between 1973 and 1985 changes in US trade flows modified factor content in a way that increased the demand for skilled relative to unskilled workers. This means that the gap between the relative factor endowment of the US economy and that of the *notional* economy increased, thereby creating upward pressure on the college wage premium. The increase in this gap was small, however (see their table VII), while the increase in the number of college graduates relative to high school graduates was substantial. They therefore concluded that "Although trade-induced changes in relative demand move in the correct direction to help explain rising education differentials in the 1980s, they are quite small relative to the increase in the relative supplies of more-educated workers over the same period" (p. 65). In other words, foreign trade did not play a big role in the rise of the US college wage premium.[4]

In a more detailed study of the factor content of trade flows between 1980 and 1995, Borjas, Freeman, and Katz (1997) found that US trade with developed economies had a negligible impact on factor prices. For trade with less-developed countries, they found a measurable but small impact. To translate changes in factor content of trade into changes in relative factor prices, the study used estimates of the elasticity of substitution between these inputs. An elasticity of substitution between high-skilled and low-skilled workers describes the percentage increase in the relative use of skilled workers when their relative wage declines by 1 percent.

Katz and Murphy (1992) estimated the elasticity of substitution between college graduates and high school graduates to be 1.41, which means that a one percentage point decline in the relative wage of college graduates raises their relative use by 1.41 percent. The inverse of this elasticity informs us by how much a one percentage point increase in the relative supply of college graduates reduces their relative wage. With an elasticity of substitution of 1.41, the decline in the relative wage equals 0.709% (that is, 1/1.41) for every percentage rise in the relative supply. They used the same methodology to assess the impact of immigration into the United States on relative wages.

Table 3.1 reports estimates from Borjas, Freeman, and Katz (1997) using three different elasticities of substitution between college graduates and high school graduates. The middle column uses the elasticity 1.41 that was estimated by Katz and Murphy (1992). The left

Table 3.1 Contribution of Immigration and Trade with Less-Developed Countries to the US College Wage Premium, 1980–1995 (in log points)

Elasticity of substitution	2	1.41	1
Immigration	0.007	0.009	0.013
Trade	0.007	0.010	0.014
Actual change	0.191	0.191	0.191

Data source: Borjas, Freeman, and Katz (1997, table 18).

column uses an elasticity of 2, while the right column uses an elasticity of 1—two hypothetical elasticities that create a range around the central estimate for sensitivity analysis.

According to the data used by Borjas, Freeman, and Katz (1997), the ratio of wages of college graduates to wages of high school graduates increased by 0.191 log points from 1980 to 1995.[5] On the other hand, immigration and trade with less-developed countries contributed 0.009 and 0.010 log points, respectively, for an elasticity of substitution equal to 1.41. In this central case, immigration and trade contributed 5 percent each to the rise of the college wage premium. A higher elasticity of substitution converts a given shift in relative supply into a smaller modification of relative wages, which can be seen in Table 3.1 by comparing the central column with the left column that reports results for an elasticity of substitution equal to 2. But even a lower elasticity of substitution, equal to 1, which raises the impact of immigration and trade on the college wage premium, yields estimates that leave the contribution of immigration and trade small, about 7 percent each (see the right column in Table 3.1). In short, neither immigration nor trade contributed significantly to the rise of the college wage premium.

Borjas, Freeman, and Katz (1997) also estimated the impact of immigration and trade with less-developed countries on wages of high school graduates relative to high school dropouts. This relative wage increased by 0.109 log points between 1980 and 1995. Yet trade contributed only 8 percent to this rise in their central case, for which they estimated an elasticity of substitution equal to 3.1.[6] On the other hand, immigration, which consisted primarily of workers with less than a college degree, contributed 44 percent to the rise in the wage of high school graduates relative to high school dropouts. Evidently, while trade had a very small impact on wage inequality between college and high school graduates as well as between high school graduates and high school dropouts, immigration had little impact on the former but a substantial impact on the latter.[7]

It is useful to pause at this point to clarify what hides behind the elasticity of substitution that was used by Borjas, Freeman, and Katz (1997) to translate changes in quantities of high school graduates and college graduates into the relative wages of these workers. The standard definition of the elasticity of substitution between two inputs applies to a constant-returns-to-scale technology that uses these inputs to produce a well-defined product, where "constant returns" means that a proportional expansion of inputs raises output by the same proportion. In this case, the elasticity of substitution depends only on features of the technology, and it has the property that manufacturers that use this technology and seek the least-costly production methods do indeed respond to factor price changes with changes in factor employment according to this elasticity. That is, if, say, the elasticity of substitution equals 2, then a decline of 1 percent in the relative wage of skilled workers induces users of this technology to raise the relative employment of skilled workers by 2 percent.

When there are multiple sectors or multiple plants with varying characteristics within sectors, however, the *aggregate* response of relative factor use to changes in relative factor prices does not typically depend on a single technological parameter. In addition, this aggregate elasticity of substitution can differ systematically from the elasticities of substitution of the individual technologies used in production, and it is sensitive to the degree to which product prices respond to changes in input quantities.

The latter complication does not arise, of course, when an economy produces a single product with a single technology. Yet even in this case, the aggregate elasticity of substitution can differ substantially from the elasticities of substitution of individual technologies within the sector. Houthakker (1955) showed, for example, that in an industry populated by heterogeneous firms that use labor and capital and whose technologies differ in capital intensity, the elasticity of substitution between labor and capital can equal 1 at the sectoral level (a Cobb-Douglas aggregate production function) when it equals 0 in every firm (a Leontief production function).[8] Clearly, in this case all firms face the same price of the final product, so that relative prices do not change when the amounts of labor and capital vary.[9]

In estimating the elasticity of substitution between college graduates and high school graduates, Katz and Murphy (1992) used changes over time in the relative supply of college graduates and a time trend to control for shifts in the relative demand for workers. As they make clear, this procedure identifies an aggregate elasticity of substitution that is as good an approximation of the true elasticity as the approximation of the time trend is to changes in demand. Further, it is not clear from this methodology to what extent price changes induced by changes in factor supplies are captured by the estimated elasticity of substitution as opposed to the demand shifts captured by the time trend. But, as Borjas, Freeman, and Katz (1997) show, in a wide range of elasticities of substitution around the Katz and Murphy estimate, the impact of trade or immigration on relative factor rewards is small compared to the actual changes. In other words, notwithstanding all the limitations embodied in the translation of factor content into relative factor rewards, based on this methodology the robust conclusion is that globalization had a small impact on the college wage premium.

There are two channels through which changes in factor availability are typically accommodated: a reallocation of inputs across sectors and changes in the intensity with which inputs are used within sectors. In other words, the absorption of changes in factor supplies can be decomposed into within-industry and between-industry variations. When product prices do not respond to output levels, all the variation of employment takes place between sectors. In particular, an increase in the supply of low-skilled workers is accommodated by an expansion of the low-skill–intensive sector, such as footwear, and a contraction of the high-skill–intensive sector, such as computers, with no changes in factor intensities. In contrast, when product prices respond to output levels, the variation of employment consists of both within- and between-industry changes, because price changes induce changes in factor prices and changes in factor prices induce changes in factor intensities. The decomposition of the employment shift into within- and between-industry variations can also be carried out in response to other changes in the economy, such as changes in demand or in the technology. Chapter 4 discusses how this type of decomposition was used to shed light on the role of trade as opposed to technology in varying wages.

4

Trade versus Technology

IN *The Race between Education and Technology*, Goldin and Katz (2008) describe the historical evolution of US wages as a race between rising education levels on the one hand and improvements in technology that shifted the relative demand for different types of workers on the other. Rising education levels reduced the relative wages of high-skilled workers and especially the wages of college graduates relative to high school graduates. On the other hand, technological change had different effects on the desired composition of the workforce in different time periods and therefore on the relative wages of skilled workers. In the early part of the twentieth century, technological innovation reduced the relative demand for high-skilled workers, while later on it raised their relative demand. The combination of a higher supply of skilled workers due to expanding education and a lower demand due to technical change reduced their relative wages initially. Later, however, a vigorous rising demand for high-skilled workers due to technical change led to an increase in their relative wages and to a higher college wage premium despite the increase in their relative supply. And the rise of the college wage premium was exacerbated by a slowdown in the growth of the number of college graduates relative to high school graduates.

This narrative identifies technological change as an important driver of inequality in the late twentieth century. But how much of the increase in the relative demand for high-skilled workers was due to technology, and how much was due to trade? To answer this question, we need to understand how technological change affected the demand for different types of workers, both directly within industries and indirectly through international specialization.

FORMS OF TECHNICAL CHANGE

Technical change is considered an improvement if it brings about higher output levels for given combinations of inputs. Such improvements can take many forms. If a technological advancement raises output at the same rate for every combination of inputs, the change in technology is said to be Hicks-neutral, in honor of the Oxford economist John Hicks. But not all technological improvements are of this type. Hicks (1932) proposed a definition of *biased* technical change that is related to the response of relative factor demands to a technological advancement.

To understand this definition, suppose that output of a particular product, say garments, is produced with skilled and unskilled workers only, under conditions of constant returns to scale. Then a manufacturer of garments who seeks the least-costly input combination in order to produce a particular output level chooses to employ skilled relative to unskilled workers based on their relative wages only. The higher the relative wage of skilled workers, the fewer skilled workers she employs relative to unskilled workers; and this employment ratio does not depend on the desired output level.

Under the Hicks definition, an improvement in technology is *low-skill saving* if it raises the demand for high-skilled relative to low-skilled workers for *given* relative wages. And an improvement in technology is *high-skill saving* if instead it raises the relative demand for low-skilled workers for given relative wages. We can therefore think about the first form of technical change as *high-skill biased* and about the latter as *low-skill biased*. This definition of factor-biased technical change can be expanded to richer production structures.

Both neutral and factor-biased technological improvements raise total factor productivity (TFP), because they raise output for given levels of inputs. In the Hicks-neutral case, an improvement in a technology coincides with a proportional increase in TFP; while in the case of factor-biased technical change, the proportional increase in TFP is related in a more complicated way to the form of technical change.

An alternative definition of factor-biased technical change, called *factor-augmenting* technical change, is more commonly used, however. Under this definition, high-skill–augmenting technical change refers to an improvement in the production technology that makes skilled workers more productive by raising *proportionately* the "effective" number of such workers. Thus, for example, if the high-skill–augmenting technical change amounts to 5 percent, this means that a given number of skilled workers operating the new technology contribute to output as much as 5 percent more than skilled workers would contribute to output with the old technology. This 5 percent skill-biased improvement in technology would be reflected in TFP growth equal to the share of skilled workers in costs times 5 percent. Thus, for example, if the share of skilled workers in wages is 40 percent, TFP would increase by 2 percent. The result would be similar for technical improvements that are low-skill augmenting. Furthermore, due to constant returns to scale, technical change that raises the productivity of both low- and high-skilled workers by 5 percent is equivalent to Hicks-neutral technical change that raises total factor productivity by 5 percent.

The two definitions of factor-biased technical change—factor-saving and factor-augmenting—are not equivalent. In particular, skill-augmenting technical change may be low-skill saving or high-skill saving under the Hicks definition. That is, a modification of the technology that makes skilled workers proportionately more efficient can lead to an increase or a decrease in the demand for high-skilled relative to low-skilled workers for given relative wages. Which way relative demand shifts depends on the elasticity of substitution between these two types of workers. When the elasticity of substitution is larger than 1, *skill-augmenting* technical change is *low-skilled-labor saving* under the Hicks definition, and it is *high-skilled-labor saving* when the elasticity of substitution is lower than 1.

Besides factoral biases, technological improvements can exhibit sectoral biases. That is, technical change can be uneven across sectors, advancing faster in some and slower in others. These sectoral biases play a distinct role in setting wages, as we shall see below.

Some technological discoveries change business practices dramatically. This was true with the invention of the steam engine and with electricity, which led to far-reaching improvements in the organization of production (see the discussion of general purpose technologies in Helpman 1998). It has also been true with the more recent advances in information and communication technologies that enable firms to fragment and reorganize the production process in ways that were not available before. Computer-aided design and computer-aided manufacturing allow firms to outsource and offshore many tasks that were traditionally performed in integrated plants. This led to rapid growth of foreign trade in services (particularly in business services), the expansion of international trade in intermediate inputs for further processing or final assembly, and the extension and proliferation of global supply chains. These novel designs of world production networks have generated large trade flows that take place both at arm's length and within the boundaries of multinational firms (see Helpman 2006; and Antràs 2016, chap. 1). As might be expected, these developments have introduced new channels through which globalization affects wages and inequality.

PRICES AND TECHNOLOGY

We have seen in Chapter 2 how changes in relative prices of final goods modify the wages of low-skilled relative to high-skilled workers. The logic of that analysis can be extended to more complicated frameworks, in which there are multiple types of labor and capital, various types of materials, and various intermediate inputs. The factor proportions theory spells out how price changes due to foreign trade are related to changes in factor rewards. To use this theory to estimate the impact of trade on wage inequality, we need estimates of the price changes caused by trade and measures of factor intensities in the affected sectors.

Lawrence and Slaughter (1993) estimated the relationship between sectoral skill intensity, measured as the employment of nonproduction relative to production workers, and price changes. They found no evidence that during the 1980s prices of high-skill–intensive products increased in the United States more than prices of low-skill–intensive products.[1] Leamer (1998) tracked sectoral prices relative to the overall producer price index during three decades: the 1960s, 1970s, and 1980s. Textiles and apparel were the low-skill–intensive sectors in his sample, and he found that their relative prices declined markedly, by 30 percent, only in the 1970s. In the 1980s, when the college wage premium soared, the relative prices of skill-intensive products increased only slightly.

One could argue that the price changes in the 1970s had their biggest impact on wages only in the 1980s, because the transmission of price shocks into wages was slow. But the credibility of this argument—which is not grounded in evidence—is questionable, even if one believes, as one should, that the adjustment of wages to prices is not contemporaneous. Besides, and importantly, these studies did not isolate the price changes caused by foreign trade. Instead, they used unconditional price changes that emanated from multiple sources of variation. In other words, it is not clear to what extent the price changes Lawrence and Slaughter or Leamer studied were caused by trade in contrast to other factors, such as demand shifts or improvements in technology. However, their evidence shows that the rise in the relative price of skill-intensive products during the 1980s was modest at best.

Could these modest changes in relative prices explain the large variations in relative wages? Leamer (1998) proposed a methodology for addressing this question, explicitly accounting for the evolution of sectoral total factor productivity levels. His methodology consisted of estimating *mandated* factor price changes; that is, factor price changes mandated by the zero profit condition in competitive markets. In this approach, the price of a final good equals the marginal cost of production, while the marginal cost of production depends on factor prices and the state of technology. For this reason, the relationship between changes in the price of a product and changes in factor prices can be expressed as:

Percentage increase in the price of a product

= Weighted average of the percentage increases in factor prices

minus The percentage increase in TFP.

In this formula, TFP stands for total factor productivity, which measures the efficiency of the technology, and the weights in the first term on the right-hand side are factor shares. In addition to different types of labor, Leamer included capital and materials. This formula is exact for *small* changes, when the technology exhibits constant returns to scale.[2]

Using estimates of changes in product prices, changes in total factor productivity, and cost shares of various inputs in 450 sectors, Leamer estimated the mandated factor price changes that best approximate this formula. Comparing the mandated wage changes with the actual changes in wages then provides an appraisal of how much of the variation in wages is explained by trade, under the null hypothesis that price changes were *caused* by trade and technical change.

The formula presented above can be used to estimate mandated factor price changes by treating product price changes, TFP growth, and the weights in the first term on the right-hand side (that is, the factor shares) as data. In this case, no account is taken of possible direct impacts of productivity changes on product prices. Under these circumstances, the form of technical change, and in particular of whether it is high-skill or low-skill biased, plays no special role (although the calculation of the rate of growth of a sector's TFP depends on the factor-augmenting forms of productivity change). Once the sector-biased rates of TFP growth become available, the precise sources of the sectoral productivity improvements are not relevant. This is the sense in which sector-biased, rather than factor-biased, technical change affects wage inequality. A productivity improvement in a high-skill–intensive sector acts similarly to a price increase that raises the skill premium. For this reason, Leamer (1998) considered different degrees to which sectoral productivity improvements might have affected prices. In one case, he assumed that falling costs due to productivity growth reduced product prices by the rate of TFP growth, the case of *full pass-through*; while in the other case, he assumed that productivity growth did not affect product prices, the case of *no pass-through*.

In one methodology, workers were categorized as high-wage earners (skilled) and low-wage earners (unskilled); while in another, they were categorized as nonproduction (skilled) and production (unskilled) workers. Leamer found that the degree of pass-through played a significant role. In the division of workers into high-wage versus low-wage earners, or nonproduction versus production workers, the 1970s estimates showed a positive impact of product price changes on wage inequality. For this reason, Leamer termed the 1970s the "Stolper-Samuelson decade."

No such clarity emerged in the 1960s nor in the 1980s. In the latter decade, which is of particular interest, the results depend on the method used to classify workers as skilled or unskilled. When workers were categorized as high-wage earners and low-wage earners, the annualized wage increases were 2.98 percent for high-wage workers and 2.89 percent for low-wage workers under the no pass-through specification, and 1.91 percent for high-wage workers and 2.75 percent for low-wage workers under the full pass-through specification (see Leamer 1998, table 4.7). Attributing these wage changes to trade therefore implies that trade had no measurable impact on wage inequality in the 1980s if there was no pass-through of technical change into prices, and it *reduced* wage inequality if the pass-through was 100 percent. In any case, these estimates cannot explain the dramatic rise of the college wage premium.

In a second methodology, where workers were grouped into production and nonproduction categories, the comparable figures are an annualized wage increase of 3.45 percent for nonproduction workers and 2.51 percent for production workers under the no pass-through specification, and 1.33 percent for nonproduction workers and -0.86 percent (a decline) for production workers under the full pass-through assumption (Leamer 1998, table 4.8). According to these estimates, trade contributed to an increase in wage inequality in the 1980s under both pass-through specifications, yet this contribution was small compared to the rise in the college wage premium. Feenstra (2015, pp. 87–91) used the same methodology to estimate the wages of nonproduction relative to production workers for the years 1979 through 1990. In one case, he accounted for sectoral TFP growth using data with and without the computer industry (because the computer industry was an outlier); and in another case, he disregarded TFP growth altogether (see Feenstra 2015, table 4.1). He concluded that the results are troubling, because "they do not reflect the actual changes in wages that occurred in the United States during the 1980s, and are quite sensitive to the data used and specification of the regression." Apparently, Stolper-Samuelson effects were not large enough to account for the rise of wage inequality in the 1980s.

Adding up the mandated wage changes from trade and technology yields results that also fall short of explaining the rise of inequality in the 1980s. According to Leamer's (1998) estimates, the combined annualized wage increases were −1.91 percent (a decline) for high-wage workers and 2.75 percent for low-wage workers under the no pass-through specification, and −1.59 percent (a decline) for high-wage workers and 3.07 percent for low-wage workers under the full pass-through assumption (Leamer 1998, table 4.7). Alternatively, for the production versus nonproduction classification of workers, the comparable figures were 1.33 percent for nonproduction workers and −0.86 percent (a decline) for production workers under the no pass-through specification, and 1.65 percent for nonproduction workers and −0.54 percent (a decline) for production workers under the full pass-through specification (Leamer 1998, table 4.8). Evidently, in the former case, of high-wage versus low-wage workers, the combined effects foresee a decline in wage inequality, in contrast to the evidence. In the latter case, of nonproduction versus production workers, the combined effects foresee a rise in wage inequality, but not large enough to explain the data.

An important lesson from this analysis is that estimates that attribute to technical change wage movements that are not explained by foreign trade may overstate the role of technology in rising inequality. Direct estimates, which use information on product price changes and elasticities of factor rewards with respect to product price changes, are admittedly hard to come by; but they are essential for a reliable decomposition of wage movements into their component parts.

LOCAL VERSUS GLOBAL TECHNOLOGICAL CHANGE

Katz and Murphy (1992) concluded that the rise of the US college wage premium during the 1980s was most likely caused by skill-biased technological change. This conclusion was based partly on the observation that the majority of the shift in relative labor demand occurred within, rather than between, sectors. What this means is that the increase in the overall employment of college graduates relative to high school graduates was mostly absorbed via an expansion of employment of college graduates relative to high school graduates within sectors, rather then to a shift of employment from less skill-intensive to more skill-intensive sectors. If, alternatively, a decline in the relative price of low-skill–intensive products had been the foremost cause of the rise in the college wage premium, we would have observed a reallocation of labor from low-skill–intensive to high-skill–intensive sectors. In addition, the resulting rise in the relative wages of skilled workers would have discouraged manufacturers from employing high-skilled workers and would therefore have resulted in a *decline* in the employment of high-skilled relative to low-skilled workers within the manufacturing industries, contrary to the evidence.

These conclusions gained support from Berman, Bound, and Griliches (1994), who studied the evolution of employment and the wage shares of production and nonproduction workers in US manufacturing sectors. They found that between 1959 and 1987, the rise in the share of nonproduction workers in employment and their wagebill share accelerated, reaching 0.552 percentage points per annum for the former and 0.774 percentage points per annum for the latter between 1979 and 1987 (compared to 0.069 and 0.051, respectively, between 1959 and 1973). Further, 0.387 out of the 0.552 percentage points were due to within-industry changes in employment. Namely, the within-industry changes accounted for about 70 percent of the rise in the employment share of nonproduction workers. They concluded that these findings are consistent with a dominant role for biased technological change but not with a dominant role for economic elements that shift product demand, such as trade or the defense buildup.

To provide direct evidence for the role of technological change in shifting labor demand toward nonproduction workers, Berman, Bound, and Griliches correlated changes in the wage share of these workers with two indicators of technology: the share of computers in investment and the share of research and development (R&D) expenditures in sales. According to their data, the share of computers in total investment almost tripled between 1977 and 1987, from 2.69 percent to 7.36 percent (see their table VII). And this rise in computer investment was positively correlated across manufacturing industries (after controlling for other variables, such as the capital–output ratio) with the rise in the share of nonproduction workers in the total wage bill. R&D investment was also positively correlated with the rise in the wage-bill share of nonproduction workers. This direct evidence was supposed to add credence to the argument that the US shift in employment from production to nonproduction workers was related to skill-biased technological change, which would also be consistent with the rise in the wages of skilled relative to unskilled workers.

Not according to Leamer (1998, 2000), however, who advanced the argument that what matters for relative wages is the *sector* bias rather than the *factor* bias of technological change. Although this is an authentic conclusion from Leamer's analysis, it rests on the premise that technological change does not modify product prices, which raises the question whether the circumstances of the 1980s are reasonably approximated by this assumption. The answer to this question is No.

The assumption of constant product prices would be satisfactory if we were examining a small country that has no impact on the prices of goods, which are determined on world markets. In contrast, this assumption is not appropriate when considering a country that is an influential player in some industries, or when the improvements in technology are not confined to a single country. The latter case is of particular interest. As information technology progressed, it was quickly adopted by many rich countries, followed by middle-income countries. Moreover, this technology changed business practices in many manufacturing sectors across the world, with different degrees of influence on sectoral productivity levels. Such broad-based changes could not have happened without affecting product prices. For this reason, a relevant analysis has to factor in the response of price changes to changes in the technology. This point was forcefully made by Paul Krugman.

Krugman (2000) developed a model of the world economy in which technological change takes place simultaneously in every country. He then showed that, contrary to sector-biased technical change, factor-biased technical change *alters* relative factor rewards.[3] In particular, if technological change is production-worker saving according to the Hicks definition, and therefore nonproduction-worker biased, then—accounting for the price responses—the relative wage of nonproduction workers will increase. And importantly, the skill premium will rise regardless of whether the technological improvement is in the low-skill–intensive or the high-skill–intensive sector. In other words, in this case the response of relative wages does not depend on the sector bias of technological change; it depends only on the factor bias of the technological improvement. All in all, widespread skill-biased technical change can raise the skill premium and increase the employment of high-skilled relative to low-skilled workers in every industry, in line with the evidence.[4]

Was skill-biased technical change ubiquitous? A positive answer to this question would suggest that an analysis of technological change that accounts for price responses is more relevant than an analysis that assumes constant prices, and therefore that the predictions of the former are more reliable as guides to what happened in reality. Indeed, the evidence points to an affirmative answer to this question. Berman, Bound, and Machin (1998, pp. 1246–1247) stated:

> In this paper we claim that skill-biased technological change was pervasive over the past two decades, occurring simultaneously in

most, if not all, developed countries. Thus, *it was not only the major cause of decreased demand for less-skilled workers in the United States, but also shifted demand from less-skilled to skilled workers throughout the developed world.* (emphasis in original)

First the authors showed that in the United Kingdom, a country that had similar economic features to those of the United States, the shift in the composition of employment between production and nonproduction workers was similar to that in the United States. While, as reported above, in the United States the annual increase in the share of nonproduction workers amounted to 0.552 percentage points between 1979 and 1987, of which 0.387 percentage points were due to within-industry changes, in the United Kingdom the corresponding numbers were 0.367 and 0.301, respectively, between 1979 and 1990 (see their table I). Second, they calculated the increased percentage of nonproduction workers in manufacturing employment, and the percentage of that increase due to within-industry changes, in ten OECD countries during the 1980s. Figure 4.1 portrays the share of the within-industry components for eight of these countries.[5] Sweden had the lowest share, 60 percent, while Belgium had the highest, 96 percent. It is evident from this figure that in all these countries the shift from the employment of production to nonproduction workers took place predominantly within, rather than between, sectors. The authors also showed that the within-industry rise in the employment of skilled workers was positively correlated across countries, and that the industries that experienced the largest shift toward nonproduction workers were associated with the spread of information technology: electric machinery, other machinery including computers, and printing and publishing.

Considerable evidence shows that advances in technology shifted factor demand toward highly skilled workers. Sectors with faster increases in the demand for such workers were more innovative, more intensive in R&D, and more intensive in computer use. Berman,

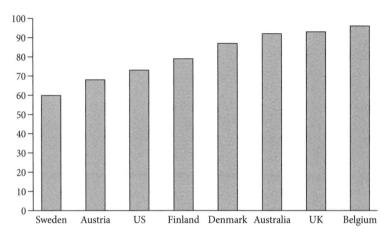

Figure 4.1 Percent of the within-sector contribution to the rise in the fraction of nonproduction workers in manufacturing employment, 1980–1990. *Data source:* Berman, Bound, and Machin (1998, table II).

Bound, and Griliches (1994) and Autor, Katz, and Krueger (1998) showed this for the United States, while Machin and Van Reenen (1998) showed comparable evidence for the United States, the United Kingdom, France, Germany, Denmark, Sweden, and Japan. Further, Machin and van Reenen found that in the seven OECD countries in their sample, the share of imports originating from less-developed countries played a minor role in explaining the rise in the employment share of skilled workers within industries. This evidence suggests that skill-biased technical change, rather than foreign trade, was more likely responsible for the rise in wage inequality between skilled and unskilled workers.

Berman and Machin (2000) analyzed changes in the wage-bill shares of production and nonproduction workers in rich, poor, and middle-income countries. They showed that in the 1980s the within-industry contribution to increases in nonproduction workers' wage-bill shares was large in all twelve rich countries in their sample with the exception of Sweden, and that changes in sectoral nonproduction workers' wage-bill shares were positively correlated across these countries. For nine of them, the upswings in their wage-bill shares were positively correlated with the US upswings, and only Austria and Belgium had a few negative correlations with other countries (see their table 2). Berman and Machin also showed that during the same time period, the within-industry contribution to the increase in nonproduction workers' wage-bill shares was large in all of the eighteen middle-income countries in their sample, with the exception of Korea, as well as in the seven poor countries in their sample, with the exception of Bangladesh. Furthermore, sectoral skill upgradings in the poor and middle-income countries were positively correlated with skill upgradings in the US sectors (see their table 4), and sectoral skill upgradings in all these countries—rich, middle-income, and poor—were positively correlated with US computer usage and OECD R&D intensity (see their table 5).

Evidently, changes in technology were widespread and exhibited similar patterns in countries at different levels of development. For this reason, it is not possible to attribute to trade all price changes in the world economy; technical change also affected product prices. This still leaves open the question of whether globalization affected technical change, which will be discussed in Chapter 9. But it is also worth bearing in mind that many of these studies, which attributed to technical change rather than to trade the rise in the skill premium, interpreted the evidence in light of a simple and highly aggregative model of international trade. As we will see in Chapter 5, and in the review of the work of Burstein and Vogel (2017), this might have been too restrictive.

5

Offshoring

TECHNOLOGICAL CHANGE has affected differentially the productivity of various factors of production, raising especially the productivity of high-skilled labor since the late 1970s. Furthermore, massive improvements in information and communication technologies (ICTs) have reduced the costs of fragmenting fabrication activities and brought about a major shift toward foreign sourcing by business firms. Improvements in communication, computer-aided design, and computer-aided manufacturing played key roles in these developments, enabling manufacturers to dissect production into stages that can be geographically separated. As a result, some parts of a manufacturing chain can be located in different regions of the home country, where the corporate headquarters are located, while other parts can be offshored to disparate countries with favorable cost conditions (see Helpman 2011, chap. 6). These developments, which Baldwin (2016) described in detail, terming them the "second unbundling," affected factor prices in developed and less-developed countries alike.[1]

Offshoring followed two common forms: arm's-length trade and foreign direct investment. In both cases, it has entailed purchases of business services, the acquisition of intermediate inputs, and the assembly of final products or product components. Johnson and Noguera (2017) provided estimates of the ratio of value added by home country in exports relative to home country's gross exports, referred to as the VAX ratio. The inverse of this index provides a measure of offshoring, because it is higher when more *imported* intermediate inputs are embodied in exports. For this reason, growth of trade in intermediate inputs leads to a decline in the VAX ratio and to an increase in its inverse.

The time trend of the inverse of the world's manufacturing VAX ratio—our measure of offshoring of manufactured products—is reported in Figure 5.1 for the years 1970 through 2008.[2] A similar trend would be found in a plot depicting the inverse of the VAX ratio for aggregate trade, which in addition to manufacturing includes agriculture, nonmanufacturing, and services, because the upward trend in manufacturing dominates the evolution of the aggregate index. The main point to note from this figure is that this index increased only modestly until the 1990s but increased rapidly thereafter until the financial crisis of 2008. Variation across countries was considerable, however (see Johnson and Noguera 2017, table D2). And in the United States, offshoring increased substantially during the 1980s, when the college wage premium soared (see below).

Has the fragmentation of production that enabled offshoring been consequential in shaping factor prices and inequality? Before addressing this question, it is important to realize that contrary to popular perception, some forms of offshoring may operate to the benefit of low-skilled workers and contribute to narrowing the wage gap between high- and low-skilled workers in the offshoring country. A particularly stark illustration of this theoretical possibility was provided by Grossman and Rossi-Hansberg (2008), who envisioned a large number of tasks that have to be performed in the manufacturing of a final product. Some of these tasks needed to be performed by high-skilled workers, while other tasks had to be performed by low-skilled workers. Further, tasks could be ranked by the difficulty

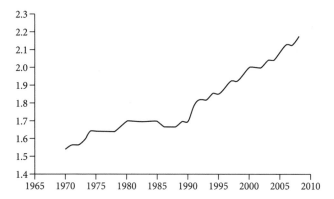

Figure 5.1 Index of offshoring manufacturing products in the world economy, 1970–2008. *Data source:* The inverse of VAX for manufacturing in Johnson and Noguera (2017, table D1).

of offshoring; some tasks could be moved at lower cost than others to foreign countries, due to differences in the relative prominence of communication and monitoring costs. These tasks were combined in different proportions in various sectors to produce final output. In a rich country with high wages, an incentive exists to offshore tasks to a less-developed country where wages are lower, especially tasks whose costs of offshoring are low. More tasks would be offshored the larger the wage gaps between the developed and less-developed countries and the lower the cost of offshoring. Technological improvements that reduce the cost of offshoring therefore would induce the offshoring of more tasks to lower-wage countries.

How does an improvement in technology that lowers offshoring costs affect the wage gap between high- and low-skilled workers in a rich country? Following Grossman's and Rossi-Hansberg's offshoring model, first consider the case in which only tasks performed by low-skilled workers are offshorable, in which case this technological change triggers more low-skill tasks to be shipped abroad. They showed that this leads to three effects. First, productivity improves among low-skilled workers in the home country, because the additional tasks that are dispatched to lower-wage countries are of lesser productivity at home compared to the remaining tasks. Second, because this reorganization of production saves low-skilled labor services, more low-skilled labor becomes available for other uses, which acts like an increase in the supply of low-skilled workers. And finally, the resulting decline of production costs lowers prices. The last two effects are similar to the effects of price changes and shifts in labor supply on relative wages, which were discussed in Chapters 2 and 3. I therefore focus now on the novel productivity effect.

In a small country that faces externally dictated prices of products, there are no price effects. In addition, changes in labor supply that do not affect the set of industries with positive output levels do not modify wages, because they are absorbed by sectoral output adaptations without amendments to factor intensities. In other words, in a small country, only the productivity effect can modify wages. When the tasks are skill-level-specific and only low-skilled tasks are offshorable, technological change that reduces the cost of offshorability acts like low-skilled-labor–biased technical change. If similar tasks are needed in high-skill– and low-skill–intensive sectors, this low-skilled-labor–biased technical change makes low-skilled workers more productive by raising proportionately the effective labor hours in all their occupations. If this rise is, say, 2 percent, then the wages of these workers rise by 2 percent, while the wages of the high-skilled workers do not change. As a result, wage inequality declines.

This is a powerful result. It flies in the face of a common view that offshoring necessarily brings about the loss of certain types of good blue-collar jobs in rich countries, which harms low-skilled workers, because it identifies circumstances in which low-skilled workers gain from the offshoring of tasks in which they specialize. There are of course additional considerations that bear on this issue, which are absent from this analysis.[3] But these do not detract from the potential sway of this productivity effect. In a similar vein, the offshoring of

tasks performed by high-skilled labor raises the wages of skilled workers via a productivity effect. For this reason, the empirical evaluation
of the role of offshoring in shaping wages has to be mindful of the extent to which technological change that reduces the cost of offshoring
affects differentially tasks performed by low-skilled and high-skilled
workers.

Evidence on the impact of offshoring to China on American demand for low-skilled and high-skilled workers was provided by
Wright (2014). His study focused on the labor supply and productivity effects of Grossman's and Rossi-Hansberg's offshoring model
(2008). Although the direct effect of offshoring reduces labor demand
and displaces workers, the productivity effect raises the demand for
labor by inducing an output expansion. The empirical question was
how large was each of these outcomes, and what was its net impact on
employment during 2001 through 2007, following China's accession
to the World Trade Organization (WTO)?

Wright estimated that a one percentage point increase in offshoring led to a direct decline in low-skilled (production workers')
labor hours by 0.29 percent, which amounted to 19 percent of the
decline in employment of this type of worker in US manufacturing
during that period.[4] At the same time, a one percentage point increase
in offshoring led to an output expansion of about 1 percent, which
increased the employment of low-skilled workers by close to 70 percent of the decline caused by the direct effect. As a result, the net
decline of employment as a result of offshoring amounted to approximately 6 percent of the actual decline in employment of production
workers. Given that during the period from 2001 through 2007 the
employment of production workers in US manufacturing shrank by
1.2 million, the two effects combined gave rise to an employment
decline of 69,000 workers, a small number relative to the total job
losses.[5]

Studying the employment effects of offshoring on high-skilled
(nonproduction) workers, Wright (2014) found no significant direct

effect. On the other hand, he estimated that offshoring indirectly increased employment of these workers slightly, through the output expansion caused by higher productivity. The actual employment of high-skilled workers in US manufacturing declined by 17.5 percent during that period, somewhat smaller than the decline in employment of low-skilled workers but substantial nevertheless. Evidently, this decline cannot be explained by Wright's estimates of offshoring channels.[6]

An alternative theory of offshoring was developed by Feenstra and Hanson (1996). Their aim was to show that similar patterns of wage changes in rich and poor countries do not necessarily contradict a foreign trade–based explanation of the rise in the college wage premium. True, the evidence of rising skill premiums in rich and poor countries alike is at odds with the implications of the traditional factor proportions trade theory. Yet Feenstra and Hanson (1996) developed a thoughtful modification of this theoretical model in order to *qualitatively* square it with the evidence.

To this end, Feenstra and Hanson envisioned the production process as a collection of many tasks or intermediate inputs that differ in factor intensity. In these circumstances, rich countries, with a high relative wage of low-skilled workers, find it profitable to source low-skill–intensive tasks and intermediate inputs from poor countries, where they are cheaper to produce. When technological change reduces the cost of offshoring, or when transport costs of intermediate inputs decline, a country with a high relative wage of low-skilled workers offshores more tasks and intermediate inputs to poorer countries, in which the wage of low-skilled workers is low. This reshaping of the sourcing pattern can take place within firm boundaries by multinational corporations, as suggested by Feenstra and Hanson, or at arm's length, as suggested by Zhu and Trefler (2005). In either case, the additional offshored tasks and intermediate inputs are least skill-intensive in the rich country and most skill-intensive in the poor. As a result, the demand for high-skilled labor rises relative to low-skilled labor in each country, bidding up the relative wage of high-skilled workers in both. Moreover, when the tasks, intermediate inputs, and final product belong to the same sector in the statistical classification, the expansion of offshoring raises the measured skill intensity of that sector in both countries. Under these circumstances, relative wages of skilled workers rise and so does the average use of high-skilled relative to low-skilled workers within industries. For this reason, this amended model could conceivably explain the data.

Does the empirical evidence support this line of reasoning? And is it quantitatively adequate? Feenstra and Hanson (1997) used data on the surge in foreign direct investment (FDI) in Mexico in the early 1980s to study the response of the wages of nonproduction relative to production workers and their relative employment. This upswing in FDI was caused by a policy change of the Mexican government, which removed a variety of restrictions on foreign investment. A large share of the FDI inflow was used to create maquiladoras, that is, foreign-owned assembly plants that exported their output. Multinational companies in the United States were the source of most of this capital inflow, and they erected maquiladoras primarily along the US–Mexico border that imported intermediate inputs from the United States and shipped back assembled products. Feenstra and Hanson found that foreign direct investment was positively correlated with the rise of the share of nonproduction workers in Mexico's wage bill; in regions with larger foreign investment, the wage share of these workers increased even further. Figure 5.2 shows the average annual change between consecutive time periods (times 100) in the share of nonproduction workers in the total wage bill in five Mexican regions.[7] From 1985 to 1988, the most dramatic increase took place in the region along the US border, represented by the thick graph in the figure, where FDI was most prominent.

The correlations in Feenstra and Hanson (1997) do not comprise hard evidence in favor of their offshoring theory. Nevertheless, those correlations are suggestive, adding credence to the mechanism

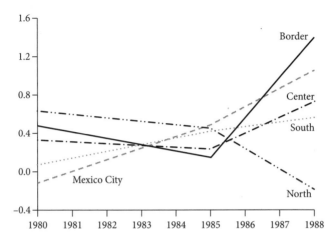

Figure 5.2 Annual average change between the current and preceding year times 100 in the share of Mexican nonproduction workers in total wages: 1975 is the preceding year to 1980, 1980 is the preceding year to 1985, and 1985 is the preceding year to 1988. *Data source:* Feenstra and Hanson (1997, table 2).

embodied in their storyline. Further, this evidence covers only half of the implications, those concerning outcomes in the destination country offshored to. What about employment and wage effects in the source country, for which the theory includes predictions too?

These predictions were addressed in Feenstra and Hanson (1999), who first pointed out that the role of imported intermediate inputs increased significantly in the United States during the 1980s. When averaged across all four-digit standard industrial classification (SIC) industries, the share of imported intermediate inputs relative to total expenditure on nonenergy intermediates increased in manufacturing from 5.3 percent in 1972 to 7.3 percent in 1979 to 12.1 percent in 1990. For their preferred alternative measure of offshoring (which they called outsourcing), computed with purchases of intermediate inputs only in the two-digit SIC industry in which the good was produced (rather than all purchases of intermediate inputs), they found

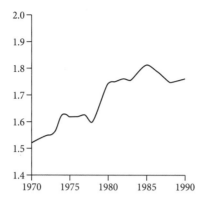

Figure 5.3 Index of offshoring manufacturing products in the United States, 1970–1990. *Data source:* The inverse of VAX for manufacturing in Johnson and Noguera (2017) online data appendix.

that the share of imported intermediates increased from 2.2 percent in 1972 to 3.1 percent in 1979 to 5.7 percent in 1990. Figure 5.3 confirms the rapid rise of offshoring in US manufacturing industries during 1979 through 1990, using an alternative index: the inverse VAX ratio from Johnson and Noguera (2017).[8] This index rose rapidly until the financial crisis of 2008.

Using a more reliable procedure than Leamer's (1998) for estimating mandated wage changes, Feenstra and Hanson estimated the impact of offshoring and high-tech capital on the relative wages of nonproduction workers.[9] Figure 5.4 presents their results. The height of each bar depicts the estimated average annual increase in nonproduction workers' relative wage caused by changes in offshoring and technology. The lower portion of each bar portrays the contribution of offshoring, while the upper part portrays the contribution of technology.

Each bar represents estimates based on a different measure of technology, in the form of computer and other high-tech capital shares. Bar I represents capital shares that were computed using data from

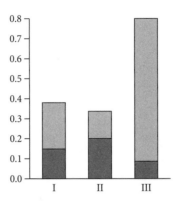

Figure 5.4 Estimated annual rates of increase in wages of nonproduction relative to production workers in percent for different measures of computers and high-tech capital: United States, 1979–1990. The lower bar represents the impact of offshoring while the upper bar represents the impact of computers and other high-tech capital. *Data source:* Feenstra and Hanson (1999, table VI).

the Bureau of Economic Analysis (BEA) in which capital services were evaluated with ex-post rental prices for computers and other high-tech capital. Bar II represents estimates in which capital shares were computed using BEA capital services evaluated with ex-ante rental prices for computers and other high-tech capital. Finally, Bar III represents estimates in which capital shares were computed using Census investment flows data for computers and other high-tech capital. Unlike the first two bars, the third gives precedence to the most recent vintages of computers and other high-tech capital. Giving extra weight to the more recent vintages is desirable in situations of rapid technological improvement, as was the case in the 1980s, although placing all the weight on the flow of investment most likely exaggerates this correction.

Each stacked bar in Figure 5.4 should be compared to 0.72, which is the average annual percentage increase in the relative wage of nonproduction workers between 1979 and 1990. From this comparison, we conclude that offshoring plus technology explains approximately half of the rise in the skill premium in the first two cases, with offshoring playing a somewhat bigger role in the second. Although offshoring explains around 20 percent of the rise in the skill premium in the former case, it explains around 27 percent in the latter. In Bar III, which is based on investment flows of computers and other high-tech capital, offshoring explains only 12 percent of the rise in the skill premium, while technology contributes close to 100 percent. Evidently, these estimates are sensitive to how one measures the value of computers and other high-tech capital, making it hard to draw strong conclusions from this study. Using a simple average of the three estimates, we find that offshoring explains close to one-fifth of the annual rise in the skill premium; a sizable share, but not overwhelming.

By 2000, the prevalent view among labor economists was that wage inequality increased primarily due to technological change (for example, Katz and Autor 1999); while trade economists adopted a more nuanced view, attributing to offshoring some of the enlargement in wage gaps. Yet it was clear to scholars in both fields that the traditional approach to international trade failed to explain the lion's share of the rise in inequality in the 1980s. In response, new research reconsidered this episode, and new evidence on the evolution of inequality emerged in later years. These developments are discussed in Part II of the book.

PART II

BROADENING THE CANVAS

IN RESPONSE to the failure of the traditional approach to account for the rise in wage inequality, scholars examined a multitude of other mechanisms that could link trade to inequality, in the hope of giving globalization a better chance to explain the data. This endeavor was driven partly by a nagging feeling that trade must have played a bigger role in the surge in inequality than that shown by the estimates, and partly by new insights from data analysis and new developments in trade theory that uncovered novel avenues through which trade could affect wage gaps. Although some of these avenues have remained largely in the realm of theoretical possibilities, others have been quantified. The basic features of these mechanisms and their application to trade and inequality are examined in the following chapters. As will become clear from these chapters, current research uses a wide range of analytical and empirical methods to address the relationship between globalization and inequality, including reduced-form estimation and quantification via simulation of structural models.

In Chapter 6, I examine the impact on wages of the sorting of heterogeneous workers to sectors and the matching of these workers with firms of varying characteristics within sectors. This is followed by a discussion in Chapter 7 of how geographically localized labor markets shape the earnings of different types of workers. In Chapter 8, I discuss the roles of product differentiation and firm heterogeneity in technology usage in affecting wages. In Chapter 9, I examine how technology choice and technical change directed by market forces can alter the relationship between trade and wages. Finally, in Chapter 10, I discuss labor market frictions that produce a distribution of wages among workers with similar attributes.

6

Matching Workers with Jobs

AS WE WILL SEE in this chapter, international trade can affect the matching of workers with firms and thereby influence the distribution of earnings. The mechanisms that link matching with inequality and those that link trade to matching are the primary concerns of this chapter.

Matching plays a central role in various economic activities. It has been used to study such problems as the assignment of firms to locations, of students to schools, of doctors to hospitals, or of workers to firms. Becker (1973) applied matching theory to marriages. An important result of his analysis, which has broad applicability, concerns the conditions under which there is positive assortative matching (PAM). This condition requires complementarity (explained below) between the two sides of a match, and PAM means that higher-valued "females" are paired with higher-valued "males," where the terms *females* and *males* are used as generic descriptive terms of two sides of a match. More generally, when Becker's condition is satisfied, better firms are assigned to better locations, better students are assigned to better schools, better doctors are assigned to better hospitals, and better workers are assigned to better firms.

For illustrative purposes, suppose that there are a fixed number of females and a fixed number of males, and the number of the former equals the number of the latter. Further, both women and men can be ranked by a single characteristic from low to high. A marriage consists of one pair, a man and a woman. Every pair produces a value based on the characteristic of the male and the characteristic of the female, and this value is higher the higher the attribute of either one of the marriage partners.

What types of matches maximize aggregate value? Becker showed that if the value of a match exhibits complementarity, then positive assortative matching maximizes the aggregate value of marriages; that is, the male with the highest value of the masculine characteristic is matched with the female with the highest feminine characteristic; the man with the second highest masculine characteristic is matched with the woman with the second highest feminine characteristic; and so on, until the man with the lowest masculine characteristic is matched with the woman with the lowest feminine characteristic. Complementarity means here that the increase in the value of a match when the masculine characteristic is replaced with a higher one is larger the larger the feminine characteristic is in the match. In other words, the marginal gain from an improved masculine characteristic is increasing in the attractiveness of the female. And symmetrically, the marginal gain from an improved feminine characteristic is increasing in the attractiveness of the man. This property is also known as *supermodularity*. Becker then showed that in a "competitive" marriage market, in which every participant seeks to maximize his/her own reward, the resulting pairings satisfy PAM.

To illustrate, consider a simple numerical example. There are two females with characteristics 1 and 2, and there are two males with characteristics 1 and 2. When a male and a female match, they produce a surplus equal to the *product* of their characteristics. As a result, a match between a 1 and a 1 produces a surplus of 1, a match between a 1 and a 2 produces a surplus of 2 independent of whether the 1 is a male or a female, and a match between a 2 and a 2 produces a surplus of 4. Under PAM, the male with characteristic 1 is matched with the female with characteristic 1, producing a surplus of 1, while the male with characteristic 2 is matched with the female with characteristic 2, producing a surplus of 4. As a result, the aggregate surplus equals 5. The only other possible matches are for the female with characteristic 1 to match with the male with characteristic 2 and for the female with characteristic 2 to match with the male with characteristic 1. This would produce two marriages, each with a surplus of 2, and therefore a surplus of 4 in the aggregate, which is smaller than the aggregate surplus under PAM. In this example, the complementarity arises from the fact that an extra unit of the characteristic of one spouse raises the surplus by an amount equal to the characteristic of the other spouse.[1]

The same logic can be applied to matching workers with jobs in different types of firms. All we need is to identify a worker characteristic, say ability, and a firm characteristic, say its managerial quality or the sophistication of its technology, in order to study the matching of workers with firms. An important difference between these types of matches and those in the marriage market is that while one male is typically matched with one female in a marriage, many workers are matched with a single firm. For this reason, models of worker–firm matches often use a stronger notion of complementarity in order to portray earnings inequality in unambiguous terms. They assume that the *natural logarithm* of the value of a match exhibits a Becker-type complementarity between the ability of the workers and the firm's sophistication. This property is also known as *log supermodularity*, which implies that a high-ability worker is *relatively* more productive compared to a low-ability worker when using a sophisticated technology compared to a simple technology.[2]

Log supermodularity has the following critical implication. Suppose, for concreteness, that workers with ability levels within a given interval, measured in appropriate units, are matched with firms whose technological sophistication levels are located in a well-defined interval, measured in appropriate units. Then log supermodularity ensures that workers with higher ability are matched with more-sophisticated firms. In particular, workers with the lowest ability match with firms whose technological sophistication is the lowest, while workers with the highest ability match with firms whose technological sophistication is the highest. In this event, more-able workers are paid higher wages, and the rate at which wages rise with ability depends on how strong is the complementarity between worker ability and firm sophistication. The rate of wage increase determines in turn wage inequality: The faster wages rise with ability, the more unequal is the wage distribution.

Now suppose that as a result of a change in the economic environment (for example, in the product price), workers with abilities in this interval match up with more-sophisticated firms; that is, *every* worker gets a job in a more-sophisticated firm (except, possibly, for the most- or least-able workers). Then the wage gap between every pair of workers with different ability levels rises. That being the case, wage inequality becomes larger.[3]

This illustrates an important property of economies in which workers match with jobs: Shifts in matching reshape the structure of wages and thereby inequality. Economic changes that improve the workers' matches raise earnings disparity, while changes that deteriorate the workers' matches reduce earnings disparity. For this reason, globalization can affect the wage distribution through its influence on the assortative matching of workers with jobs. The jobs can involve matching with different types of equipment, different types of managers, different types of firms, or different types of sectors. As long as log supermodularity prevails, better matches for workers lead to more wage inequality.

These ideas have been used to study the influence of trade on wage disparities. They make possible the examination of inequality at different parts of the wage distribution, comparing, for example, shifts in inequality at the top end with shifts in inequality at the bottom

Table 6.1 Earnings Inequality in OECD Countries

	2000		2007		2014	
	5/1	*9/5*	*5/1*	*9/5*	*5/1*	*9/5*
Canada	2.00	1.80	1.99	1.89	1.95	1.90
France	1.53	2.01	1.49	2.00	—	—
Germany	1.71	1.79	1.83	1.78	1.87	1.82
Ireland	1.70	1.92	1.86	2.03	1.98	2.00
Japan	1.62	1.84	1.65	1.86	1.60	1.84
Korea	2.02	2.00	2.03	2.46	1.98	2.42
Norway	1.41	1.42	1.52	1.47	1.62	1.50
Sweden	1.39	1.69	1.40	1.67	—	—
United Kingdom	1.84	1.93	1.81	1.98	1.80	1.98
United States	2.05	2.19	2.11	2.31	2.09	2.40

Decile ratios of gross earnings.
Data source: OECD.Stat, accessed on August 16, 2016.

end of the distribution in response to globalization. Analytical frameworks of this type, which embrace rich heterogeneity among workers, are needed for understanding patterns of change in earnings inequality in countries with varying experiences, in which inequality changed in different ways along the distribution of earnings.

Table 6.1 shows ratios of the 5th to the 1st decile and the 9th to the 5th decile of earnings in a number of OECD countries in 2000, 2007, and 2014 (unfortunately, this data set does not contain earlier years). The former ratio measures inequality at the lower part of the distribution, while the latter ratio measures inequality at the upper part. The most interesting comparison is between 2000 and 2007, both years before the financial crisis, because 2014 reflects to some degree the impact of the Great Recession on earnings inequality.

First, note that there is substantial variation in inequality in these data. Between 2000 and 2007, inequality increased in some countries at the bottom as well as at the top of the distribution (that is, both ratios decile 5/decile 1 and decile 9/decile 5 increased). These include Ireland, Japan, Korea, Norway, and the United States. On the other side, inequality declined at the bottom and increased at the top in Canada and the United Kingdom, and it increased at the bottom and declined at the top in Germany and Sweden. Finally, in France, inequality declined at both ends. Evidently, these countries have seen substantially different shifts in inequality at different segments of their distribution of earnings.

Inequality further increased from 2007 to 2014 at the bottom of the distribution in Germany, Ireland, and Norway, but not in Japan or the United States. And it further increased from 2007 to 2014 at the top of the distribution in Canada, Norway, and the United States, but not in Ireland, Japan, Korea, or the United Kingdom.

In the United States, for which longer-term data is available, the shifts in the upper and lower tails of the distribution of earnings changed significantly over time. Using data from the Social Security Administration, Kopczuk, Saez, and Song (2010) showed that between 1939 and 2004, the 50/20 and 80/50 percentile ratios of earnings of men followed a U-shaped pattern, falling initially and rising eventually (see their figure II). However, although the two ratios where strongly positively correlated during most of that period, in the 1990s the top ratio increased and the bottom ratio declined for much of the time. This reduced middle-range earnings relative to both the top and bottom percentiles, thereby leading to wage polarization. These diverse experiences motivate the need to study the entire profile of income changes.

Needless to say, workers are heterogeneous, and trade affects the wages of different types of workers differentially. Whereas most of the discussion so far has focused on two types of workers, skilled and unskilled, the matching mechanism can encompass richer patterns of worker heterogeneity, with implications for wage inequality across the entire spectrum of earnings. Some of these implications are explored in the rest of this chapter.

Costinot and Vogel (2010) developed a variant of the factor proportions trade model that features multiple sectors and multiple types of workers, in which markets are competitive and workers are sorted into sectors (they use the terminology that workers match with sectors).[4] One interpretation of their model is that sectors produce intermediate inputs that are traded internationally, and every country uses these intermediates to assemble its own final consumer goods. Another interpretation is that workers are matched with tasks (that is, a sector is relabeled to be a task), and the tasks are combined to produce a final product. In the latter case, a country relies on tasks performed in other countries for the fabrication of its own final consumer and investment products. This interpretation might be appropriate, for example, for trade in business services. However, workers differ in a single dimension—we will call it ability; Castinot and Vogel call it skill—and the productivity of a worker with a given ability varies across sectors. Critically, the productivity of a worker with a specific ability level depends only on her sector of employment; it does not depend on how many or what type of other workers are employed in this industry. In addition, sectors can be ordered by a single characteristic, say technological sophistication, so that the natural logarithm of output per worker, which depends on the worker's ability and the sector's sophistication, exhibits complementarity. That is, labor productivity is log supermodular in worker ability and firm sophistication. In these circumstances, there is positive assortative matching: Higher-ability workers match with more-sophisticated sectors in every country.

In this world, international trade has an unambiguous effect on wage inequality when the countries differ in factor endowments in a way that exhibits a strong ranking of relative ability abundance.[5] This means the following: Suppose that the world consists of two countries; and for any two ability levels, one country has relatively more workers with the higher ability (this is known as the monotone like-lihood ratio property). In this case, we can state unambiguously that this country is high-ability abundant compared to the other. Costinot and Vogel showed that the opening of trade between two such coun-tries improves matches for all workers in the high-ability-abundant country and worsens them for all workers in the low-ability-abundant country. That is, in the skill-abundant country, trade leads to a re-allocation of labor across sectors so that every worker is employed in a more-sophisticated industry, and the opposite happens in the other country. As explained above, when workers are matched with more-sophisticated sectors (or firms), the gap in wages between every higher-ability and every lower-ability worker rises, leading to more wage inequality. It follows that trade *raises* wage inequality in the high-ability-abundant country and *lowers* wage inequality in the low-ability-abundant country. These results are similar in spirit to the implications of the simple two-sector factor proportions trade model with low-skilled and high-skilled workers, in which the opening of trade benefits the relatively abundant factor in each country, leading to a higher relative wage of skilled workers in the skill-rich coun-try and to a lower relative wage of skilled workers in the skill-poor country.

Trade alters matching in more complex situations as well. Of par-ticular interest is trade between countries that differ in the *diversity* of factor endowments (what Costinot and Vogel call North–North trade).[6] For concreteness, suppose that there is an ability level such that one country is high-ability abundant above this skill level and low-ability abundant below this skill level compared to the other country. Then it is reasonable to think of the former country as having a more diverse factor endowment. This is a particular way in which endowments differ across countries, but it proves to be instructive for the purpose at hand. Costinot and Vogel showed that in these cir-cumstances, trade worsens the matches of low-ability workers and improves the matches of high-ability workers in the country with a more diverse factor endowment, and the opposite occurs in the country with the less diverse factor endowment. As a consequence, wage inequality declines at the lower end of the wage distribution and rises at the upper end of the wage distribution in the more diverse country, and the opposite happens in the less diverse country. This illustrates an important point: Although globalization may raise or reduce a country's inequality along the entire wage spectrum, it may also affect inequality differently at different ability intervals. Evidently, structural features of the world economy play a key role in these outcomes, and theory can identify their differing impacts.

The last point comes out even more strongly in Grossman, Helpman, and Kircher (2017), who studied a two-sector economy that employs two factors of production: workers and managers. In their setup, factor intensity differs across sectors so that one sector is worker intensive and the other is manager intensive. Unlike the standard model, however, both workers and managers are heterogeneous, with varying ability levels. As a result, there are two types of matches: matches of inputs with sectors and matches between inputs within sectors. In other words, certain types of workers and managers are employed in the worker-intensive sector, and the other workers and managers are employed in the manager-intensive sector. At the same time, within every sector workers of varying abilities match with managers of varying ability levels. To distinguish the matching of inputs with sectors from the matching of inputs within sectors, the authors use *sorting* to describe the former and *matching* to describe the latter.

The total factor productivity of a firm that employs a manager with workers who share a common ability level is higher the higher the ability of either the manager or her workers. The productivity function is log supermodular; and it depends on only the attributes of the workers and the manager, notwithstanding the fact that there is diminishing marginal productivity in the *number* of workers per manager.[7] Furthermore, although individual firms have no incentive to mix the abilities of managers or workers, every sector employs workers and managers with multiple ability levels.

The types of workers and managers employed in each sector depend on technological features and product prices. Through product prices, international trade affects the sorting of inputs to sectors. By affecting sorting, trade affects the composition of the workers and managers employed in each sector and thereby the matching that takes place there. Within every sector, the matching pattern determines in turn the inequality of wages and managerial earnings. Although log supermodularity of productivity ensures positive assortative matching within every sector, sorting across sectors does not necessarily satisfy PAM. In other words, in every sector, firms with better managers employ better workers; but if, say, a group of the best managers sorts into the exporting sector, it is nevertheless possible for a group of the least-able workers to sort into the exporting sector as well. Sufficient conditions for the best managers to sort to the same sector with the most-able workers, or the best managers to sort to the sector with the least-able workers, are provided in Grossman, Helpman, and Kircher (2017). These conditions are expressed in terms of cross-sectoral comparisons of factor intensities and features of the productivity functions. In this environment, elements from the factor proportions theory interact with matching and sorting in determining the impact of globalization on inequality.

As motivation for considering these types of configurations, Grossman, Helpman, and Kircher (2017) report in their online appendix evidence from Brazil, using data from Helpman, Itskhoki, Muendler, and Redding (2017). These data distinguish among five occupations and twelve manufacturing sectors. One occupation consists of managers and other professional workers, while the other four consist of different types of white- and blue-collar employees. Aggregating the latter four occupations into a single category of workers, Figure 6.1 presents the 1994 correlation between the mean wages of workers and the mean earnings of managers across twelve manufacturing sec-

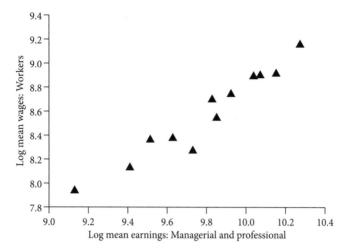

Figure 6.1 Relationship between mean wages of workers and mean earnings of managers in twelve manufacturing sectors, Brazil 1994. *Data source:* Helpman, Itskhoki, Muendler, and Redding (2017).

tors in Brazil. Evidently, in these data, sectors with higher earnings of managers also pay higher wages to workers, suggesting that more-able workers sort to sectors with more-able managers. A similar pattern is exhibited in Figure 6.2 for Sweden in 2004. Although the Swedish data has fourteen manufacturing sectors, the average wages of workers and earnings of managers were constructed from five occupations, comparable to Brazil.[8] In Sweden, too, more-able workers appear to sort to sectors with more-able managers.

In view of this evidence, I focus the following presentation of Grossman, Helpman, and Kircher's (2017) analysis on an economy in which the best workers and the best managers are employed in one industry, while the least-able workers and managers are employed in the other. The analysis showed that this sorting pattern arises when the following two elasticity ratios are higher in the same sector: (1) the elasticity of output with respect to the ability of managers, relative to the elasticity of output with respect to the quantity of managers; and

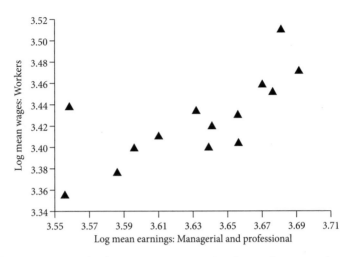

Figure 6.2 Relationship between mean wages of workers and mean earnings of managers in fourteen manufacturing sectors, Sweden, 2004. *Data source:* Anders Akerman via private communication.

(2) the elasticity of output with respect to the ability of workers, relative to the elasticity of output with respect to the quantity of workers. When this condition holds, the best workers and the best managers sort to the industry in which these elasticity ratios are the largest.

First consider the case in which factor intensities do not differ much between the sectors, in which case the sectoral differences in the above-described elasticity ratios are driven by the elasticities of output with respect to ability. How will inequality change when globalization changes product prices? Suppose, for example, that it raises the price of the product produced by the industry with the least-able factors of production. Then inequality of earnings across sectors declines, as would be predicted by the factor-specific trade model (see Helpman 2011, section 3.3).[9] There is indeed an element of factor specificity in this framework that emanates from the sorting pattern. This is because the least-able factors of production are somewhat specific to their sector of employment, as are the most-able factors of

production, since they sort according to their comparative advantage
in producing these goods. This quasispecificity is responsible for the
narrowing of the inequality of earnings between the sectors.[10]

In addition, there is rematching of workers and managers in every
industry. More workers and managers are attracted to the low-ability
sector in response to the price hike. But this means that the range
of abilities expands together with the number of employees in the
low-ability sector and contracts in the high-ability sector, because
the former sector attracts the least-able workers and managers from
the latter sector and these employees are more able than the low-
ability sector's original employees. This resorting applies to both
workers and managers. Grossman, Helpman, and Kircher showed
that given similar factor proportions in the two sectors, this improves
matching for one factor of production (be it workers or managers) in
both sectors, and matching deteriorates in both sectors for the other
factor of production (see their proposition 6). Consequently, within-
sector compensation inequality rises in both sectors for the input
whose matching has improved and declines in both sectors for the
input whose matching has deteriorated. Under these circumstances,
globalization that raises the relative price of goods produced by low-
ability workers and managers leads to a negative correlation between
the within-sector inequality of wages and managerial earnings; and
it narrows the earnings disparities between sectors. Symmetrically,
globalization that raises the relative price of goods produced by high-
ability workers and managers leads to a negative correlation between
the within-sector inequality of wages and managerial earnings; but it
widens earnings disparities between sectors.[11]

Grossman, Helpman, and Kircher (2017) reported in their online appendix that the changes in the inequality of worker wages and
managerial earnings between the years 1986 and 1994 were weakly
negatively correlated across the twelve Brazilian manufacturing sectors depicted in Figure 6.1, in line with the above prediction. To
construct this correlation, they used data on price changes provided

by Marc Muendler (private communication) and worker wages and managerial earnings from Helpman, Itskhoki, Muendler, and Redding (2017). Since Brazil liberalized trade in 1991, when it joined the free trade area MERCOSUR, a significant part of the price changes between 1986 and 1994 can be attributed to this policy. It can then be argued that this illustrates a case in which globalization generated a negative correlation between changes in the inequality of compensation for workers and managers across manufacturing sectors. This type of result requires a conceptual framework that can encompass the rich heterogeneity of factors of production that are involved.

Sectoral differences in factor intensity open the door to interesting variations. Suppose, as above, that globalization raises the price of goods manufactured by the sector with the least-able employees. Then, the quasispecificity of inputs still leads to a reduction of income disparity between sectors; the low-ability sector expands by hiring more workers and managers whose abilities are higher than the abilities of its original employees; and the high-ability sector contracts by shaking off its least-able workers and managers. Now, however, the resulting rematching of workers and managers within sectors does not have to improve the matches of one party across the board. If indeed matches improve for labor in one sector and deteriorate in the other, then the former sector has to be labor intensive. And similarly for managers.[12] In this case, factor intensity interacts meaningfully with matching, unveiling the sector in which a factor's matching improves. Improved matching raises the within-sector inequality of a factor's compensation, while deteriorated matching reduces its within-sector inequality. For this reason, globalization raises wage inequality in the labor-intensive sector and dampens it in the management-intensive sector, so that within-sector inequality is negatively correlated between workers and managers, between workers in different sectors, and between managers in different sectors (see their proposition 7).

Matching between workers and managers is also analyzed in Antràs, Garicano, and Rossi-Hansberg (2006). In their framework, there is a managerial hierarchy. Every manager has a team of workers. The ability of a worker determines the range of production problems he can handle. If he encounters a problem that is outside this range, he forwards it to his manager and she solves the problem if it happens to be in the range that she can handle. Solving a problem requires a fixed amount of time on the part of the manager. Every person can handle problems whose upper bound is determined by her ability, and therefore more-able individuals can solve all the problems that less-able individuals can solve, and more. A problem without a solution prevents the worker from contributing to output. This structure produces a complementarity between the ability of the worker and the ability of the manager.

Individuals are heterogeneous in ability, and ability is continuously distributed. There is a single sector that produces homogeneous output by teams of workers and managers. The economy is competitive, yielding positive assortative matching between workers and managers: Better workers are matched with better managers. And since higher-ability individuals have a comparative advantage in management, the highest-ability individuals sort into management and the rest become production workers. The resulting matches generate a wage distribution among production workers and a distribution of earnings among managers.

Starting with two closed economies, say North and South, Antràs, Garicano, and Rossi-Hansberg examined the impact of globalization on wage and earnings inequality. In autarky, workers match with managers that reside in their own country; whereas in a globalized world, workers in one country can match with managers in another country. As a result, globalization leads to a rematching of workers and managers around the globe, a form of offshoring, which changes the distribution of income.

When the ability distributions are uniform between zero and an upper bound, and one country has a larger upper bound, it is natural to refer to the latter as North and to the former as South. When other things are the same in these countries, globalization can lead all individuals in South to be employed by northern managers. And because the southern workers have the lowest abilities, they work for the lowest-ability managers in North. Alternatively, depending on parameter values, some southern individuals can be managers in a globalized world. In this event, the least-able individuals in South are employed by southern managers, while the most-able individuals in South are employed by the best northern managers. However, in all cases, southern workers improve their matches.

Focusing on the absolute difference in wages of the highest- and lowest-ability workers as a measure of inequality, Antràs, Garicano, and Rossi-Hansberg showed that globalization raises wage inequality within the group of southern workers. It also raises wage inequality within the group of northern workers if management consumes little time and the skill gap between North and South is large. Otherwise, globalization reduces wage inequality among northern workers. Moreover, globalization reduces earnings inequality among southern managers but has ambiguous effects on earnings inequality among northern managers.[13]

QUANTITATIVE EVALUATION

A detailed quantitative study of wage determinants in the US economy, which incorporates workers with multiple attributes that sort into multiple occupations and are paired with two types of equipment, is provided in Burstein, Morales, and Vogel (2016). Their study combines sorting of labor and equipment across occupations and matching of workers with equipment within occupations. Occupational services are combined to manufacture consumption goods and equipment.

The theoretical model encompasses a rich structure of comparative advantage of different types of workers in the use of equipment and employment in diverse occupations, as well as comparative advantage of equipment in these occupations. Within each worker-type group, there is heterogeneity in overall productivity between individuals and in their relative productivity across equipment and occupations.[14] Based on these attributes, competition leads to sorting and matching, the formation of "prices" of occupations (that is, their values in production), and a distribution of wages. International trade alters the demand for different types of occupations, leading to resorting of workers and equipment across occupations and their rematching within occupations. As a result, the valuation of occupations changes and so does the structure of wages. Technical change that reduces equipment prices also leads to a revaluation of occupation services and thereby affects wages.

To illustrate, consider an increase in the demand for the services of a particular occupation, say "Technicians and related support" (which is one of their occupation categories). This raises the value of this occupation and thereby the relative wages of labor-type groups that are disproportionately employed in this occupation. More-complex relationships arise, however, when the price of one type of equipment declines, say "Computers" (which is one of their equipment categories). On impact, this reduces the relative costs of occupations that use computers intensively and raises the demand for labor-type groups that use computers intensively. Accordingly, the relative wages of *labor-type groups* that use computers intensively rise, while the relative "prices" of *occupations* that use computers intensively decline on impact. The latter exerts in turn downward pressure on the relative wages of labor-type groups that are intensively employed in *computer-intensive occupations*.

In the empirical analysis, Burstein, Morales, and Vogel (2016) used thirty occupational categories, which in addition to "Technicians and related support" include "Engineer," "Executive, administrative, managerial," "Health diagnosis," "Retail sales," and "Food preparation and service," among others. Equipment had two categories: "Computers" and "Other equipment." Workers were divided into thirty groups, sorted by gender, five education levels, and three age brackets.[15] Computer usage provides an explicit channel through which technology affected wage inequality, because the spread of personal computers was uneven across occupations as well as across workers with different characteristics within occupations; it was biased toward more-educated workers and toward women. A rapidly falling price of computers, a reflection of technological change, encouraged growth in the adoption of computers in the workplace, which affected in turn the composition of labor demand and the structure of wages, as explained above. On the supply side, a rising relative supply of more-educated workers also affected the composition of employment and wages, along familiar lines discussed in Chapter 2.

Between 1984 and 2003, the log of the skill premium, defined as the average wage of workers with a college degree relative to those without a college degree, increased in the United States by 15.1 log points (see table 3 in Burstein, Morales, and Vogel, 2016).[16] This skill premium would have declined by 11.4 log points due to changes in labor supply had there been no changes in labor demand. Yet shifts in labor demand increased the skill premium by 26.5 log points. About 60 percent of this demand effect was due to computer usage, and 18.5 percent was due to shifts in demand for different occupations. Labor productivity accounted for the remainder of the demand shift, where labor productivity was estimated as a residual. The large impact of computers on the skill premium emanated from two sources: the comparative advantage of educated workers in computer use, and the comparative advantage of educated workers in computer-intensive occupations. For example, in 1984 the share of hours worked with computers was 45.5 percent by individuals with a college degree and 22.1 percent by individuals without a college degree. In 2003, these numbers were 85.7 percent and 45.3 percent, respectively. And in both years, the share of hours worked with computers was larger for women than for men.

To assess the impact of globalization on the skill premium of US workers, Burstein, Morales, and Vogel (2016) examined how trade affected demand for all categories of workers. They found that if the American economy had had no access to international markets for equipment (including computers), then the 2003 skill premium would have been lower by 2.2 percentage points; and if the US economy could not have traded occupation services, the 2003 skill premium would have been lower by 6.5 percentage points. Comparable figures for 1984 were 0.1 percentage points for no trade in equipment and 5.2 percentage points for no trade in occupation services (see their tables 7 and 8). Therefore, trade in equipment raised the skill premium by 2.1 percentage points, and trade in occupation services raised it by 1.3 percentage points between 1984 and 2003. Since the actual rise in the skill premium during that period amounted to 28 percentage points (see Autor 2014), these findings suggest that international trade had a modest impact on wage inequality in the United States.

Lee (2017) provided an analysis of wage inequality that accounts for trade relationships among multiple countries. Her economies have multiple sectors and multiple occupations. Comparative advantage across countries emanates from sectoral productivity differences and varying compositions of worker types. Within every group of workers that belong to the same type, individuals differ in productivity across occupations and sectors. The distributions of these productivity levels are worker-type dependent.[17] Based on these individual attributes, every worker sorts into a specific occupation-sector cell that offers her the highest income. As Lee emphasized, sorting into occupations in addition to sorting into industries plays an important role in her findings.

In Lee's quantitative analysis, there were thirty-two countries, and the rest of the world was aggregated into a thirty-third country. The countries included rich economies, such as the United States, the United Kingdom, and Japan, as well as middle-income economies, such as Argentina and Brazil. Workers were grouped into five categories, based on education level: high school dropouts, high school graduates, workers with some college education, college graduates, and workers with advanced degrees. Sectors were composed of agriculture, mining, manufacturing, and services. Occupations were aggregated into five groupings, based on required skills and routineness of the occupational tasks. The lowest in the ranking was "Low-Skill Occupations," while the highest was "Managers, Professionals, and Technicians." Unlike Burstein, Morales, and Vogel (2016), Lee did not account for the role of capital in production. After estimating the parameters of the model, Lee (2017) carried out a number of counterfactual experiments to quantify the impact of trade on wages and sector-occupation sorting patterns.

In one counterfactual exercise, Lee analyzed changes in bilateral trade costs in agriculture, mining, and manufacturing that were chosen (calibrated) to yield within the model the factual changes in the trade flows. Between 2000 and 2007, these declines in trade costs were about twice as high in the manufacturing sector, where they declined by 12.4 percent on average, than in agriculture or mining. This lowering of trade costs, which brought about more integration in the world economy, raised the real wages of every group of workers in every country in the sample (see her table A3). Since these estimated changes were restricted to group averages, they did not speak to distributional consequences for individual workers within groups. Nevertheless, it is remarkable that this significant increase in globalization had no negative effects on high school dropouts or on any other education group, despite the operation of the Stolper-Samuelson mechanism in the economic structure. This was possible because Lee's model included Ricardian forces of comparative advantage, meaning that countries also differed in relative sectoral productivity levels.

Moreover, the response of real wages in different education groups varied a lot across countries. In many rich countries, such as Canada, Italy, Japan, Sweden, the United Kingdom, and the United States, inequality increased throughout: The gains of high school dropouts were lower than the gains of high school graduates, which were lower than the gains of individuals with some college education, which were lower than the gains of college graduates, which were lower than the gains of individuals with a post-college education. But a similar pattern also emerged in some of the poorer countries, such as China, India, Indonesia, Poland, and Turkey. In other countries, the pattern of real wage gains exhibited a U-shape across the education groups, rising more for high school dropouts and post-college degree earners than for the other workers. This nonmonotonic response was estimated for Argentina, Brazil, Greece, Israel, and the Netherlands. Of particular note is the observation that in all these countries except Greece, high school dropouts gained the most. And there were two countries, New Zealand and Switzerland, in which the gains in real wages were monotonic, but with larger gains for lower-educated workers (see Lee's figure A4). In this experiment, inequality increased in some countries and declined in others; yet these changes were not correlated with development levels.

The above results were used to calculate the contribution of lower trade costs to the college wage premia, by comparing average wages of workers with some college education or more with the average wages of high school graduates and high school dropouts.[18] They implied that the lower trade costs explain only 11.4 percent of the rise in the college wage premium in the United States between 2000 and 2007, and only about 17 percent of the rise in the college wage premium in China. We see again that expansion of trade, driven by falling trade costs, explains only a fraction of the rise in the reward to skill. Lee also pointed out that in some European countries, such as Italy and Spain, the skill premium declined after 2000 despite the upward pressure from lower trade costs (see Lee's figure 2). The declines reflected the dominance of rising supplies of college graduates.

Another experiment examined the impact of an across-the-board productivity improvement in China, amounting to 11.2 percent. This

Table 6.2 Rise in US Real Wages: 2000–2007 (in percent)

Worker type	HD	HG	SC	CG	AD
Decline in trade costs	1.15	1.15	1.49	1.62	1.81
Rise in China's productivity	0.06	0.09	0.13	0.14	0.17

Worker types: high school dropouts (HD), high school graduates (HG), some college education (SC), college graduates (CG), and advanced degrees (AD).
Data source: Eunhee Lee, private communication.

productivity improvement is based on estimates from Hsieh and Ossa (2016). The resulting changes in real wages were much smaller in this case than those resulting from the decline in trade costs.[19] Table 6.2 illustrates this difference for the United States, where the trade-costs reduction affected real wages ten to twenty times more than did the improvement in China's productivity. These size differences are typical for other countries as well.

An important difference between the results of the China productivity rise and the decline of the trade costs is that China's productivity gains hurt labor groups in a number of countries. Although China's surge raised real wages of all groups in many countries, real wages declined in all five groups of workers in Chile and Indonesia. In some countries, the results were mixed, with higher real wages for some worker types and lower real wages for others. In Argentina, for example, real wages of high school dropouts declined by 0.18 percent while real wages of more-educated workers increased. In Brazil, real wages of high school dropouts declined by 0.11 percent and increased for all more-educated workers. Nevertheless, all these changes were small and had therefore only small effects on inequality. In summary, according to this study, neither the decline in trade costs nor China's productivity surge had a large impact on inequality between 2000 and 2007.

7

Regional Disparity

MY DISCUSSION has so far emphasized inequality across groups of workers with varying characteristics, but these characteristics did not include domicile traits except for country of residency. The implicit view in this approach is that similar individuals who reside in the same country experience comparable labor market outcomes. To justify this view, it is typically assumed that every individual can costlessly seek employment within the borders of his own country, but not in other countries. Evidently, this approach excludes international migration from the analysis and takes an extreme stand on *internal* migration.

There is, however, substantial evidence that labor mobility is limited not only across international borders but also across regions within countries. Moreover, the degree of internal mobility is not uniform; that is, it has been low in India, Brazil, and Germany and relatively high in the United States (see Topalova 2007, for India; Kovak 2013, for Brazil; Autor, Dorn, and Hanson 2013, for the United States; and Dauth, Findeisen, and Suedekum 2014, for Germany). Nevertheless, even in the United States labor mobility has been limited across states and across smaller geographic zones within states. These observations gave rise to an interest in the impact of globalization on regional inequality on the one hand and inequality across different types of workers within regions on the other. Further, although studies of regional effects of globalization did not always rely on explicit theoretical frameworks, and some that did differed in details, they all shared two important assumptions: First, that workers who reside in a country's subregion do not change their domicile in response to globalization or trade liberalization; and second, that globalization and trade reforms affect regions differentially because of dissimilarities in sectoral composition. Some sectors are more affected by tariff cuts, which are typically not uniform during trade liberalization, or by surges of exports from trade partners, whose comparative advantage is concentrated in certain industries. As a result, the average impact on a country's state, province, or district depends on the sectors located in the area and the distribution of employment across these sectors (for example, steel in Pennsylvania and coal mining in West Virginia). Differences in sectoral composition foster differences in outcome.

To understand an important mechanism through which regional wages are differentially affected by globalization, consider a country in which workers are attached to regions, but every worker can costlessly seek employment in any sector operating in his region. Under these circumstances, the wages of similar workers have to be the same in a region, independently of their sector of employment, but wages can vary across regions. In the extreme case in which within a region all workers are alike, wage inequality arises only as a result of wage disparity across regions.

Assume for the time being that all workers are alike within a region and that a typical region forms an economy à la Jones (1971) with many sectors, each sector with its own sector-specific inputs, and every sector selling its products within the country as well as in foreign countries. In a regional economy, the sector-specific inputs may consist of mineral deposits, agricultural land of certain types, or capital equipment specialized to particular uses. Workers seek employment within their region in the sector paying the highest wage. As a result, the distribution of employment across sectors ensures that every sector pays the same wage rate. This distribution of employment depends on the prices of goods produced in each and every sector (with a higher price leading to higher employment), on the quantities of the sector-specific inputs available in the region (with a higher quantity of a sector-specific input leading to higher employment), and on the technologies available for production. If the technologies are the same in all regions and they all face the same prices, then geographic wage differences arise only as a result of differences in sector-specific input availability and the size of the labor force. These factor endowments are assumed to be fixed.

Now consider the impact on wages of a price decline, say in the price of garments, where the price might have changed as a result of an increase in foreign supply or a domestic trade reform that reduced the tariff on textiles and clothing. This price decline can be viewed as a common shock to all regions. How will this affect wages? Will wages decline in all areas proportionately, or will they fall at varying rates? If wages decline proportionately, then this trade shock has no impact on regional wage inequality. But if the rate of decline of wages differs across regions, then this trade shock modifies wage inequality.

Jones (1971) derived a formula that links a price shock to wage effects, and this formula was used by Kovak (2013) to study the impact of trade liberalization in Brazil on its subregional wage inequality. According to the formula, every sector is assigned an index, which I will call the Jones index, that is composed of three variables: the elasticity of substitution between labor and the sector-specific input, the share of labor employed by the industry, and the share of the sector-specific input in the industry's costs. The Jones index is constructed from these variables as follows:

$$\text{Jones index} = \frac{\text{Elasticity of substitution times labor share}}{\text{Share of the sector-specific input in costs.}}$$

Using this index, the formula implies that the impact on wages of a price fall, say by 2 percent on ceramics, is proportional to the Jones index for the ceramic industry divided by the sum of the Jones index across all sectors. Namely, it is proportional to the following response measure:

Ceramic industry response measure

$$= \frac{\text{Jones index for ceramics}}{\text{Sum of jones index across all sectors.}}$$

Obviously, this implies that the wage decline is smaller than 2 percent, but the decline is larger the larger is the Jones index of the ceramic sector relative to the other industries. When many prices change simultaneously in the course of trade liberalization, the regional decline in wages equals a weighted average of the price declines, where the weight of an industry equals the above-described response measure. Variation across regions in sectoral composition and in factor endowments generates variation across regions in the response of wages to price changes and thereby affects wage inequality.

Brazil implemented a major trade liberalization program that started in 1990 and culminated in the formation of MERCOSUR. During that period, tariffs (and tariff equivalents) declined from an average of 30.5 percent to an average of 12.8 percent. But the decline varied substantially across sectors, with large declines in "Rubber" and "Apparel" and small declines in "Petroleum, Gas, and Coal." Agriculture received a small dose of additional protection (see Dix-Carneiro and Kovak 2017, figure 1). Since the sectoral composition varied across the Brazilian microregions (more than four hundred in total), the size of the price shock, computed as the weighted average of price changes using the above-described regional weights, also varied significantly across the micro regions (see Kovak 2013, figure 3).[1] In addition, wage changes varied across the micro regions. Estimating the impact of regional price declines due to tariff changes on wages, Kovak (2013) found that a 10 percentage point larger average price decline due to trade liberalization brought about a 4 percentage point larger decline in a region's wages. The average decline of prices due to tariff cuts in regions at the 95th percentile of the 1991 wage distribution was larger by 7.6 percentage points than in regions at the 5th percentile of the wage distribution. Therefore, trade liberalization led to a drop in wages that was 3.4 percentage points greater in the former regions than in the latter. Accordingly, this episode presents a case in which trade liberalization *reduced* regional inequality.

Yet the impact of the Brazilian liberalization on regional wage inequality was small. Computing the log of relative average wages between a subregion in the 90th percentile of the geographic wage distribution and a subregion in the 10th percentile, Kovak found a value of 0.572, which amounts to 77 percent higher wages in the 90th percentile subregion.[2] On the other hand, the log of this wage ratio would have been 0.590 in the absence of trade liberalization, which amounts to 80 percent higher wages in a 90th percentile subregion. The decline of inequality between subregions in the 75th and 25th percentiles was even smaller; the log of the wage ratio was 0.299, and it would have been 0.305 without the tariff cuts. Therefore, the trade reform reduced the wage ratio between the 75th and 25th percentile subregions from 36 percent to 35 percent. Evidently, this episode of trade liberalization reduced regional wage disparity, but not by much.

Dix-Carneiro and Kovak (2015) extended the analysis to account for labor heterogeneity, combining skilled and unskilled workers with sector-specific inputs in the fabrication process (see their online appendix), where skilled workers are defined as individuals with a high school education or more, and unskilled workers are defined as workers with less than a high school education. In 1991, the wages of skilled workers were ninety-six log points higher than wages of the unskilled. Although the average skill premium remained relatively constant between 1991 and 2000, it varied significantly across the micro regions. By 2010, the average skill premium had declined to seventy-two log points and remained heterogeneous across regions.

This extension enabled Dix-Carneiro and Kovak to estimate the impact of Brazil's trade liberalization on regional skill premia. Although some of the estimates proved to be insignificant (that is, one could not reject the hypothesis that trade liberalization did not change the skill premium), other estimates suggested that the tariff cuts reduced inequality between the skilled and unskilled workers (because tariffs declined relatively more in skill-intensive sectors). Yet the final conclusion was that ". . . the differential tariff shocks can explain at most 14 percent of the 1991 through 2000 decline in the skill premium" (Dix-Carneiro and Kovak 2015, p. 556). It follows from this analysis that Brazil's 1991 trade liberalization contributed only modestly to the closing of the wage gap between skilled and unskilled workers. Other influences were responsible for more than 85 percent of the decline in the skill premium.

In a further elaboration on Brazil's trade liberalization, Dix-Carneiro and Kovak (2017) studied long-term consequences for regional wages and employment in the formal sector.[3] They found that the effects on earnings were qualitatively similar to those reported by Kovak (2013), except that the declines lasted for an extended period, accumulating until the mid-2000s. These cumulative effects were larger than the shorter-term changes identified by Kovak. Further, microregions with larger declines in prices due to tariff reductions suffered larger contractions of employment in the formal sector. These employment declines also accumulated over many years, stabilizing in the mid-2000s. Importantly, the prolonged adjustments to the trade reform were driven by the lack of labor mobility across regions, sluggish adjustment of capital (mostly via depreciation and differential investment rates), and localized agglomeration economies that bring about higher productivity in larger regions. The time horizon over which Brazil's adjustment played out is surprisingly long and highly unusual.[4] It nevertheless suggests the need to pay more attention to dynamic responses whose cumulative effects can be much larger than the short-term impacts.

Another trade reform that affected local labor markets is the 1994 North American Free Trade Agreement (NAFTA). Although estimates of NAFTA's impact on aggregate welfare were small,[5] Hakobyan and McLaren (2016) found significant regional influences of the agreement on low-skilled US workers in direct competition with imports from Mexico. Their study considered more than 500 US regions, called CONSPUMAs (Consistent Public Use Microdata Areas), which consist of county groupings that nest into states. And they applied a methodology similar to Kovak (2013) for estimating wage responses to price changes that were induced by trade liberalization, in the form of US tariff reductions between 1990 and 2000 toward imports from Mexico. Unlike Kovak, however, Hakobyan and McLaren's weighted average of price changes did not account for the sectoral variation in the costs of sector-specific inputs; and they incorporated into the weights an index of *revealed comparative advantage* (RCA) due to Balassa (1965).[6] The inclusion of the RCA index was justified as follows: ". . . a high tariff on imports of good j from Mexico makes no difference if Mexico has no comparative advantage in j and will not export it regardless of the tariff" (Hakobyan and McLaren 2016, p. 730). Although one can be sympathetic to the need to account for comparative advantage, the form in which it was introduced into this analysis was rather arbitrary. As a result of these modifications, the Hakobyan and McLaren estimation strategy does not have a clear theoretical justification and their quantitative findings have to be interpreted with caution. In view of these limitations, one can only hope that their findings nevertheless provide a sense of the strength of NAFTA's impact on local labor markets in the United States.

The estimates of wage and nonwage effects were carried out for workers with varying education levels: high school dropouts, high school graduates, some college education, and college graduates. For most workers the effects were small or insignificant, except for high school dropouts. In a CONSPUMA that lost all of its import protection by 2000, a one standard deviation increase in the above-discussed index of vulnerability reduced the wage growth of high school dropouts by 1.41 percent between 1990 and 2000. Nevertheless, in the most *vulnerable* CONSPUMAs, the drop in wage growth of these workers amounted to 8 percentage points, a much bigger impact. In addition, trade liberalization affected low-skilled workers in the vulnerable regions in both traded and nontraded sectors.

Difference-in-difference estimators are often used to assess the impact of trade on regional outcomes. In the current context, this method addresses the following types of questions: How is the *difference between two regions* in an outcome variable, such as average wages, affected by a *difference between two periods* in some measure of the foreign trade conditions, such as tariffs. Hence, the double difference. For this reason, the difference-in-difference estimates discussed so far in this chapter encapsulate only *relative* effects across areas; and they do not lend themselves to evaluations of aggregate outcomes—such as total changes in employment—without an explicit introduction of more elaborate structural features or strong assumptions (more on this below). This point was forcefully made by Topalova (2007), who was among the first to use this methodology to study regional variation in outcomes that result from a trade policy reform. Her work, including Topalova (2010), examined the impact of India's 1991 trade liberalization on poverty and inequality, exploiting regional differences in sectoral compositions. And she stated explicitly:

> It is important to note that this exercise does not study the level effect of liberalization on poverty in India but rather the relative impact of areas more or less exposed to liberalization. Thus, while liberalization may have had an overall effect on increasing or lowering the poverty rate and poverty gap, this paper captures the fact that these effects were not equal throughout the country, and certain areas and certain segments of the society benefited less (or suffered more) from liberalization (Topalova 2007, p. 293).

Topalova found that rural districts exposed to larger sectoral tariff cuts (due to their sectoral composition), weighted by employment, experienced larger increases in poverty, while districts exposed to smaller tariff cuts experienced smaller increases in poverty. But she found no relationship between the tariff cuts and poverty across urban districts. And moreover, she found no statistically significant relationship between the regional tariff cuts and regional inequality.

Hanson (2007) pointed out similar limitations of difference-in-difference methods, which he used to study changes in regional inequality in Mexico in response to its trade liberalization of the early 1980s. Estimating the distribution of labor income in Mexican states, he found that the distributions shifted to the right (that is, higher incomes became more likely) in states with a high exposure to globalization (measured by exposure to imports, foreign direct investment, and the presence of maquiladoras) relative to the distributions in low-exposure states. Further, the fraction of wage earners with income below the poverty line increased somewhat in the low-exposure states relative to the high-exposure states.

An important element of the recent globalization has been the growth of China and the rise of its prominence in the world's trading system, especially after its accession to the World Trade Organization (WTO) in 2001. The evolution of the shares of China and the United States in the world's merchandise exports is depicted in Figure 7.1. Although the United States share declined from 12.2 percent in 1973 to 9.4 percent in 2015, China's share increased from 1 percent in 1973 to 14.2 percent in 2015. The spectacular rise of China was driven by fast productivity growth and rapid industrialization.

Similarly to the United States, the share of other rich countries in world trade declined. Japan's share of merchandise trade declined from 6.4 percent in 1973 to 3.9 percent in 2015, and Germany's share declined from 11.3 percent in 1973 to 8.3 percent in 2015. On the other side, some middle-income countries held on to their trade status or even increased their trade share. Brazil's share remained within

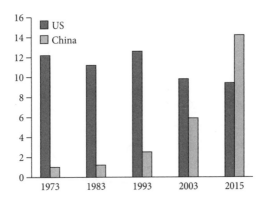

Figure 7.1 Shares of China and the United States in the world's merchandise exports (in percent). *Data source:* World Trade Organization (2016, table A4).

the vicinity of 1.1 percent during those years, while Chile's share increased from 0.2 percent in 1973 to 0.4 percent in 2015. India, another fast-growing country, increased its share from 0.5 percent in 1973 to 1.7 percent in 2015.[7]

China's rise to a world trading power was examined in multiple studies. Autor, Dorn, and Hanson (2013) investigated its impact on US geographic disparity between 1990 and 2007. Using more than 700 *commuting zones* (CZs) as the units of observation, which are smaller than the CONSPUMAs used by Hakobyan and McLaren (2016), they employed difference-in-difference methods to study the impact of China's export surge on wages, employment, unemployment, and government transfers. Similarly to other studies in this vain, their estimates identified the differential regional impacts of China's exports, using the variation across commuting zones in their sectoral composition. However, unlike the previous studies discussed in this chapter, they did not use estimates of price changes in order to construct regional trade shocks. Instead, they used trade volumes, instrumented with China's exports to rich countries other than the United States. This strategy was justified with a model of monopolistic competition à la Helpman and Krugman (1985), to be discussed in Chapter 8. In this type of model, productivity improvements in China expand the range (variety) of products fabricated in China, thereby raising exports.

The formal model, developed in the Autor, Dorn, and Hanson online appendix, does not account for unemployment; it assumes that every worker finds employment in some available occupation. For this reason, it is hard to gauge the extent to which the estimation equations are consistent with labor market frictions that lead to unemployment. Further, the main estimation equations were simplified with the aid of special assumptions, including disregard for third-country effects such as US trade with European countries, so as to arrive at a convenient form for empirical analysis (see Autor, Dorn, and Hanson's equation (2) for the employment effects). Finally, although the justification given for the rise of China's exports was a productivity surge in its manufacturing industries, the instrument for the empirical analysis did not use direct measures of sectoral productivity, but rather their potential consequences in the form of exports to other rich countries.

With regard to wages, Autor, Dorn, and Hanson (2013) found from their difference-in-difference estimates that an additional $1,000 total per worker exposure to imports from China over a decade reduced a commuting zone's mean weekly earnings by 0.759 log points (see their table 6).[8] However, when estimating separately the impacts of these differences on manufacturing and nonmanufacturing sectors, they found no effect on the wages of manufacturing workers; so that the entire attrition of earnings took place among nonmanufacturing workers, who were mostly employed in services. This result is puzzling: Because US imports from China were concentrated in manufacturing industries, their negative impact on employment was estimated to be large and concentrated in manufacturing; and there was no visible impact on nonmanufacturing employment (see their table 7).[9] Moreover, the differential decline in earnings of nonmanufacturing workers was only slightly smaller among college graduates (0.743 log points) than among noncollege graduates (0.822 log points). Autor, Dorn, and Hanson (2013) offered the following explanation for these findings:

> The fact that manufacturing wages do not fall along with employ-ment may indicate that manufacturing wages are downward rigid or that any wage effects are masked by shifts in employment composi-tion. That wages fall in non-manufacturing, however, suggests that this sector is subject to a combination of negative demand shocks—working through reduced demand for non-traded services—and positive shocks to sectoral labor supply, as workers leaving manu-facturing seek jobs outside of the sector. Overall, the findings sug-gest that general equilibrium effects operate within but not across local labor markets: an adverse demand shock to manufacturing reduces wages in other sectors locally but is not dissipated either within or across sectors in the broader (nonlocal) labor market (p. 2148).

General equilibrium effects can indeed be important for trade out-comes (see below), but they were not accounted for in this and similar studies.

Although Autor, Dorn, and Hanson found no significant effects of the China shock on differences across commuting zones' (CZ) pop-ulation levels, they did find substantially lower labor force participa-tion and higher unemployment in more-affected CZs, concentrated among workers with no college degree (see their table 5). The differ-ence between college graduates and workers with no college degree was particularly pronounced in the nonmanufacturing sector. There, a CZ's additional $1,000 total per-worker exposure to imports from China was associated with lower noncollege employment of 0.53 per-centage points and *higher* employment of college graduates of 0.17 percentage points (although the latter estimate was not significantly different from zero). They also found higher transfer payments in the more-affected zones, in the form of Trade Adjustment Assistance (TAA), Unemployment Benefits, Social Security Disability Insurance benefits, and other programs. An additional $1,000 total per-worker exposure to imports from China was associated with higher transfers of 1.01 log points, which amounted to $58 per capita.

The Trade Adjustment Assistance (TAA) program was designed to alleviate some of the damage caused by import competition, so it is not surprising that CZs more adversely affected by imports from China obtained larger transfers on account of this program. Indeed, Hakobyan and McLaren (2016) reported a similar finding: TAA benefits increased more in CONSPUMAs that were more affected by import competition from Mexico as a result of the North American Free Trade Agreement. Yet this program was small and has remained so. What is particularly striking in Autor, Dorn, and Hanson's (2013) findings is that large transfers from much bigger programs, which were not especially designed to deal with import competition, played such a prominent role in alleviating the relative distress in China-affected regions.

Autor, Dorn, and Hanson (2013) also reported estimates that accounted for US exports to China. They found that using *net* imports from China (that is, imports minus exports) rather than gross imports in the construction of the exposure index to China's trade shock reduced by 25 percent the size of the negative differential effects on manufacturing employment in the United States. Yet here, too, potentially important third-country effects were not factored in. Not accounting for exports to other countries is of particular concern due to the fact that US imports and exports evolved in tandem, despite the rise of its trade deficit (see figure 3.12 in Council of Economic Advisors, *Economic Report of the President* 2016).

A more refined view of the impact of imports from China on US wage inequality is portrayed by Chetverikov, Larsen, and Palmer (2016), who—using the Autor, Dorn, and Hanson (2013) data— examined inequality *within* CZs across twenty quantiles of the wage distribution. They found that workers in lower quantiles were more adversely affected than workers in higher quantiles (see their figure 1). Moreover, while for quantiles above the median one could not reject the hypothesis of a zero effect, the impacts were negative for lower quantiles. The biggest negative effects were estimated for the second and third quantiles, on the order of −1.4 log points, which corresponds to a 2.6 percent decline in earnings from 2000 to 2007 for the CZ exposed to the average China shock. Although significant, this relative wage decline is not very large and cannot explain the sharp rise in US wage inequality.

Countries other than the United States were also exposed to the rise of China, with different consequences. Germany is a case in point. Dauth, Findeisen, and Suedekum (2014) used the Autor, Dorn, and Hanson (2013) methodology to investigate the impact on German regions of the rapid trade expansion not only of China but also of the former members of the Soviet Union in Eastern Europe. Although imports and exports from both China and Eastern Europe were extremely small in the late 1980s, they rose rapidly in the 1990s and the 2000s. By 2008, both trade volumes had risen, but trade with Eastern Europe was more than double the volume with China (see Dauth, Findeisen, and Suedekum 2014, figure 1).

These authors found that the rise of Eastern Europe after the fall of the Iron Curtain affected German local labor markets more than did the rise of China. In sectors in which China had a comparative advantage, German imports were diverted from other countries toward China, with little displacement of production within Germany. Furthermore, German exports did not compete directly with Chinese exports. Not so for Eastern Europe, whose rising industries competed head-on with German exports. On the other side, Eastern Europe became an attractive market for German exporters who added jobs in their districts. The differential impact on wages and employment across the regions resulted from differences in sectoral composition; regions with a concentration of East European import-competing sectors fared relatively worse in terms of manufacturing and nonmanufacturing employment, while regions with a concentration of export-oriented industries fared relatively better in terms of employment in both manufacturing and nonmanufacturing industries.

Dauth, Findeisen, and Suedekum estimated that an additional 1,000 euros per worker increase over a decade of imports from the East (from both China and Eastern Europe) *reduced* a region's manufacturing employment relative to its working age population by 0.19 percentage points, while a similar increase in export exposure *increased* the regional share by 0.4 percentage points.[10] A comparable coefficient for import competition from China estimated by Autor, Dorn, and Hanson (2013) for the United States was 0.596, which goes up to 0.786 when account is taken of the difference in currencies (euros versus US dollars) and years of benchmarking (2005 versus 2007) in the two studies. Evidently, the impact of Chinese imports on US manufacturing employment variation across regions was much stronger at the margin than was the impact of imports from the East on German manufacturing employment differences across regions. Moreover, the negative marginal effect of *net* imports from China on US manufacturing employment was more than twice as high as the negative marginal effect of net imports from the East on German manufacturing employment (0.594 versus 0.237; see p. 1657). Because most of the impact of the rise of the East on Germany was due to the rise of the Eastern European countries, the impact of China on Germany was much smaller than its impact on the United States.

FROM DIFFERENCES TO AGGREGATES

How many manufacturing jobs did China's ascent destroy in the United States? How many jobs did it destroy in Germany? Or were jobs destroyed at all? The Autor, Dorn, and Hanson (2013) and Dauth, Findeisen, and Suedekum (2014) estimates cannot answer these questions, because difference-in-difference methods tell us only how many more (or fewer) jobs were destroyed in one region compared to another. If one has in addition to the difference-in-difference estimates an independent estimate of the employment impact in one particular region, then the employment outcome in this region together with the estimated variation across regions can be combined into an aggregate estimate.

To illustrate, suppose that there are three provinces in a country and the estimated differences from the impact of an economic shock on employment, using a difference-in-difference estimator, are as follows: province 2 gained 100,000 jobs more than province 1 (or lost 100,000 jobs less than province 1), and province 3 gained 300,000 jobs more than province 1 (or lost 300,000 jobs less than province 1). If we know nothing about absolute changes in employment in response to this shock, these estimates provide no information on whether the shock increased aggregate employment, reduced aggregate employment, or raised employment in one province and reduced it in another. Suppose, however, that we manage to estimate with other methods or data that there was no change in employment in province 2. Then the difference-in-difference estimates tell us that employment declined by 100,000 jobs in province 1 and increased by 200,000 jobs in province 3, so that on net there were employment gains of 100,000. Alternatively, suppose that we manage to estimate that provinces 1 and 2 together lost 200,000 jobs. Then the difference-in-difference estimates imply that province 1 lost 150,000 jobs, while province 2 lost 50,000 (100,000 less than province 1). Moreover, province 3 must have gained 150,000 jobs (which amounts to 300,000 more than province 1). Therefore, there was an aggregate job loss of 50,000. Finally, suppose that we find out that province 3, which suffered the smallest decline in employment or the largest employment gains, was not affected by this shock, so that its employment has not changed. Then the difference-in-difference estimates imply that province 1 lost 300,000 jobs and province 2 lost 200,000 jobs. In these circumstances, aggregate job losses were 500,000. Clearly, the aggregate loss of employment is larger the larger are job losses in the least negatively affected province.

Autor, Dorn, and Hanson (2013) provided a calculation of aggregate employment losses in the United States *assuming*, as in the last example above, that imports from China did not change employment in the least negatively affected commuting zone (this assumption is implicit in their calculation). They found that a $1,000 per worker increase in import exposure over a decade reduced manufacturing employment per working age population by 0.596 percentage points (p. 2139). Since the actual import exposure increased by $1,140 per worker between 1990 and 2000 and by $1,839 per worker between 2000 and 2007, they found that US manufacturing employment per population fell by 0.68 percentage points during the first period and by 1.10 percentage points during the second period. These amounted to 33 percent and 55 percent, respectively, of the actual declines in manufacturing employment during those time spells. Using the same approach, Dauth, Findeisen, and Suedekum (2014) found that the German aggregate decline in manufacturing employment per population as a result of the import surge from China and the East European countries was 1.17 percentage points over the two decades of their study, 1988 through 2008, much lower than the US estimate. How much weight to place on these aggregates depends of course on what one thinks about the reliability of the implicit assumption about the region with the relatively "best" outcome. As we have seen in the examples above, the aggregates are very sensitive to assumptions of this type.

Another method for calculating aggregate employment losses from Chinese import competition was used by Acemoglu, Autor, Dorn, Hanson, and Price (2016). Their study focused on the role of intersectoral linkages in order to account for the fact that a typical industry uses production inputs fabricated in other sectors. To achieve this aim, they centered on a sectoral-level analysis using more than three hundred industries, which allowed them to consider both the downstream and upstream relations of each of them.[11] And they showed that the estimated impacts of import competition were larger when the sectoral linkages were incorporated into the analysis.[12]

Acemoglu, Autor, Dorn, Hanson, and Price (2016) also employed a difference-in-difference analysis across commuting zones to capture effects that were beyond the purview of the sectoral-level investigation. For the latter, they divided the sectors into three categories: industries exposed to import competition, nonexposed tradable industries, and other nonexposed industries.[13] Using the Autor, Dorn, and Hanson (2013) methodology, they found that in the variation across CZs, import competition from China affected employment differences in the exposed sector but not in the two nonexposed sectors. The latter coefficients were imprecisely estimated, and one could not reject the hypothesis that they equaled zero (see their table 7). Motivated by these findings, they computed the aggregate employment effects by *assuming* that the average *absolute* impact in the nonexposed sectors was zero as well.[14] This produced an estimate of 2.4 million job losses between 1999 and 2011 (see their table 8). This estimate is quite large, and it embodies particularly large employment losses in specific areas of the country. Yet the aggregate is sensitive to the assumption of no average job gains or losses in the nonexposed sectors.

To gauge the size of this estimate, note that in the United States, manufacturing employment declined by about 6 million jobs between 1999 and 2011; and that in 1999, total manufacturing employment was 17.3 million out of a total of 129 million nonfarm payroll employees.[15] The decline in manufacturing employment took place against the backdrop of a total employment increase of 3 million between 1999 and 2011. In other words, the estimate of 2.4 million would account for 40 percent of the decline in manufacturing employment except that some of the industries in the exposed sector were outside of manufacturing. Moreover, this loss, which materialized over more than a decade, was small relative to total employment. It also was small relative to the flow of hires and separations. Lazear and Spletzer (2012) reported that in the last quarter of 2007, there were close to 12.8 million hires and close to 12.2 million separations in the US economy (see their table 1). These numbers dwarf the 2.4 million jobs lost during 1999 through 2011, which amount to an average of 50,000 jobs lost per quarter.[16] By looking at just these aggregates, one would expect the China trade shock to be easily accommodated except for the fact that the geographic concentration of industries made the adjustment painful due to limited labor mobility across regions.

STRUCTURAL QUANTIFICATION

An alternative assessment of the impact of the rise of China on regional disparities is provided by structural models. A structural model specifies all the relationships among economic actors in the economy. It is then quantified using a mix of estimated and calibrated parameters.[17] Because the model is fully specified, meaning that it covers every aspect of the constructed economy, it can be used to carry out counterfactual experiments. Specifically, it can answer the following questions: What is the impact of particular reductions in trade frictions, such as tariffs or transportation costs? Or what is the impact of a productivity surge in one country, say China, on its trade partners? We have seen in Chapter 6 how Lee (2017) used a structural model to shed light on the role matching plays in shaping inequality. However, her work did not speak to regional differences in outcomes.

The structural approach is quite different from the econometric approaches adopted in the studies discussed so far in this chapter. Its advantage is an ability to provide a glimpse into what might have been the outcomes in circumstances other than the actual ones, including aggregate outcomes. The disadvantage of this approach is that its answers are heavily dependent on modelling details, including what functions were chosen to describe production, consumption, or the statistical distribution of various variables. Although parameters of these functions are estimated or calibrated, the functional forms have to be chosen a priori. In addition, the calibration forces the model to explain particular objects (called "moments") without allowing for other excluded variables and mechanisms to play a role. As a result there is no residual variation. And finally, computational constraints often limit the size of structural models. No such commitment to detail is needed for the econometric approach. But then the econometric approach cannot be used to reliably evaluate counterfactual outcomes. Although counterfactual outcomes describe situations that were neither observed in the past nor may ever be observed in the future, they isolate the quantitative impacts of specific mechanisms. Given the advantages and disadvantages of both approaches, it is useful to examine a range of estimates obtained from each one of them.[18]

Caliendo, Dvorkin, and Parro (2015) studied regional disparities with a dynamic structural model. In this model, workers are attached to a specific sector in a specific location or they are unemployed. A worker can switch sectors and locations at a cost, which depends on the original sector-location pair and on the destination sector-location pair as well as on a random cost component specific to the worker.[19] Workers choose to stay where they are or to switch jobs depending on their assessment of future expected income in different locations and industries. Unlike the local labor markets discussed above, here workers are not rigidly attached to their locations. Instead, they face moving costs that have to be estimated.

The geography consists of the fifty US states and thirty-seven other countries (one of the other countries consisting of an aggregate of countries). There are twelve manufacturing sectors, eight service sectors, the construction sector, and wholesale and retail trade: twenty-two sectors in total. There is a sector-specific input in every sector-location pair. And every sector-location pair produces intermediate inputs using the sector-specific input and local labor as well as a final product put out by the region. The final product serves as an intermediate input as well as a consumption good. There are transport costs for shipping intermediate goods across regions. Evidently, this model cannot speak to disparity of outcomes across US commuting zones, but it can shed light on disparities across US states.

Caliendo, Dvorkin, and Parro constructed the China shock along the lines proposed by Autor, Dorn, and Hanson (2013) and used it to *infer* the sectoral productivity changes in China that would generate in the model the observed changes in US imports from China. They then ran their model with and without these productivity changes, attributing the differences between the two runs to the China shock. They found that the productivity improvements in China gradually reduced manufacturing employment relative to the downward trend that would have taken place anyway (see their figure 1).

Because the Caliendo, Dvorkin, and Parro model covered the entire world economy, their estimated responses included not only changes in US imports but also changes in US exports. According to these estimates, the Chinese productivity surge reduced manufacturing employment in the United States by an additional 0.5 percentage points over ten years, or by 0.8 million jobs. On the other side, this productivity surge increased the employment share of services, wholesale and retail trade, and construction, which more than offset the decline of employment in manufacturing. As a result, unemployment declined slightly, by 0.03 percentage points. Cheaper imports of intermediate inputs enabled the rise in employment in the nonmanufacturing sectors. These estimates paint a very different picture than the partial equilibrium estimates from the other studies.

The decline of employment in the manufacturing industries was highly concentrated in furniture, computers and electronics, metals, and textiles. This led to regional disparities in the downsizing of manufacturing industries. California, the home of a large share of the computer industry, suffered the most, followed by Texas.

Additional states that suffered substantial losses of manufacturing jobs were Pennsylvania, Illinois, and North Carolina. And there were states that suffered little, like Hawaii, Montana, North Dakota, and South Dakota (see their figure 4).

Aggregate outcomes are of little help to individual workers who lose their jobs. Although the Caliendo, Dvorkin, and Parro (2015) study built in job-switching costs across sectors and locations, it did not attempt to match employment and earnings profiles of displaced workers. Yet these profiles are important for understanding the costs borne by individuals who have been negatively affected by import competition or, for that matter, by any other economic shock that reduces earnings or forces workers to switch jobs. The study by Autor, Dorn, Hanson, and Song (2014) used individual-level data from the Social Security Administration to portray such profiles. Constructing an industry-level measure of import competition from China for the period 1992 through 2007, they found that workers who in 1991 were employed in more import-exposed industries suffered from lower cumulative earnings and lower earnings per year worked. In addition, they relied more on Social Security Disability Insurance (SSDI), similar to the findings in Autor, Dorn, and Hanson (2013) for the CZs. Although these workers were more likely to switch employers and sectors and move out of manufacturing altogether, their spatial mobility was limited.

Among workers with high attachment to the labor force (whose earnings in 1988 through 1991 exceeded the equivalent of 1,600 annual hours of work at the minimum wage), the gap in *cumulative* earnings changes during 1992 through 2007 between those employed in industries at the 75th percentile of exposure to the China shock and those employed in industries at the 25th percentile of exposure was 45.8 percent of their initial *annual* wage. This loss of earnings emanated primarily from reductions of earnings at the initial employer or at new employers in the same (two-digit) industry. Surprisingly, "employment losses are almost entirely offset: trade-impacted workers make back their employment losses in the initial firm and industry through employment outside of the original two-digit industry" (Autor, Dorn, Hanson, and Song 2014, p. 1825).

Estimating the effects on workers in different terciles of the average annual distribution of earnings during 1988 through 1991, Autor, Dorn, Hanson, and Song found that workers were more adversely affected in the lower terciles. A low-wage worker in the first tercile, employed in a manufacturing industry at the 75th percentile of exposure to import competition from China, amassed from 1992 through 2007 an additional income loss equal to 1.2 years of his initial annual earnings in comparison to a similar worker employed in a manufacturing industry at the 25th percentile of the import exposure. For workers in the second tercile, the effect was about half as large, and it was practically nil for workers in the third tercile. In other words, high-wage workers hardly suffered differential cumulative income losses in response to the rise of China.

The main conclusion from this chapter is that regional disparities were significantly affected by globalization even though inequality across groups of workers with similar characteristics changed only modestly. Moreover, the high concentration of negative repercussions of foreign shocks on some geographic areas was matched only by the high concentration of negative earnings effects among individuals who were initially employed in the most affected industries. That is, although aggregate effects were not very large, personal consequences could be substantial based on location, industry of employment, and initial earnings.

8

Firm Characteristics

IN THE RESEARCH discussed thus far, attributes of individual firms did not play a notable role. In the traditional approaches to foreign trade, sectors were the unit of analysis, and the nature of firms within industries was not specified. Combining the assumptions of constant returns to scale and firms' lack of market power enabled scholars to hone in on sectoral attributes and endowments as drivers of comparative advantage. In this way, scholars avoided the need to deal with individual firms.

Starting in the early 1980s, however, this approach was revised in response to two new sets of evidence: First, that large trade volumes took place within sectors (for example, bilateral imports and exports of garments) between countries with similar factor compositions, and second, that not only were business firms heterogeneous within industries but firm characteristics could predict participation in foreign trade (see Helpman 2011, chaps. 4 and 5). These observations revolutionized trade theory by placing business firms at the core of the analysis, and this novel approach yielded models useful for addressing a variety of substantive issues, including the relationship between globalization and inequality.

SCALE EFFECTS

While a variety of market structures were explored during the first wave of research in the early 1980s, monopolistic competition soon became the dominant trait of trade models. In this view, a typical sector is populated by firms with limited market power, which derives from product differentiation and firm-specific economies of scale (see Helpman and Krugman 1985). That is, every firm manufactures a product that is unique, be it a final good or an intermediate input, although the products are good substitutes for each other. Shirts, for example, may differ in color or style, and consumers may differ in preferences for shirts or they may just like to wear an assortment of colors and styles rather than the same type of shirt every day. As a result, there is demand for variety. Yet each brand of a product entails some fixed costs of production. These costs may arise from investment in the development of a specific design, or investment in a requisite technology for fabrication of a design, or from fixed costs associated with day-to-day operations. Many firms enter the industry as long as the fixed costs are not too large. Each one of them has its own brand, but its market power is limited by the availability of many other competing brands. The incumbent firms engage in pricing above unit fabrication costs, and the number of entrants proceed up to the point at which the operating profits of an incumbent just cover its fixed costs. In these circumstances, firms make zero profits.

These ideas were originally developed by Chamberlin (1933) and were later usefully formalized by Spence (1976) and Dixit and Stiglitz (1977). The latter introduced the constant-elasticity-of-substitution preference function for varieties of a differentiated product, and this formulation was broadly adopted in the literature. Similarly to the elasticity of substitution between high-skilled and low-skilled workers discussed in Chapter 3, the elasticity of substitution in consumer preferences reflects the responsiveness of relative quantities to relative price changes. Thus, for example, if the elasticity of substitution in consumption between black shoes and brown shoes equals 2, this means that the consumption of black shoes relative to the consumption of brown shoes declines by 2 percent when the price of black shoes relative to the price of brown shoes rises by 1 percent. The advantage of this formulation is that it yields a simple parametric representation of the elasticity of demand, which equals the elasticity of substitution. Further, this elasticity of substitution also represents an index of the love for variety: The smaller this elasticity, the less substitutable the brands of the product for each other. This is because the less responsive are relative demands to relative price changes, the more valuable variety is to consumers.

A closed economy delivers a larger array of brands—and therefore has a larger number of firms—if it is bigger (it has more inputs), the fixed costs are lower, or the elasticity of substitution is lower. And similar relationships between variety, the number of firms, economic size, fixed costs, and the elasticity of substitution arise when the brands of the differentiated product serve as intermediate inputs.

This approach was integrated into trade theory.[1] In combination with differences across sectors in factor intensities and differences across countries in factor composition, the theory produced a rich model of foreign trade. The interaction between economies of scale and monopolistic competition generated intra-industry trade and sizable volumes of trade between similar countries, in line with the evidence (see Helpman and Krugman 1985). Yet the authors of these studies *assumed* that within every sector all firms had the same technologies, independently of their brands of the differentiated product. As a result, they could not speak to questions concerning firm heterogeneity, such as the impact of trade on the size distribution of firms. Further developments designed to explore issues related to firm heterogeneity had to wait until 2003 (see below).

It was widely recognized in the 1980s that the gains from trade are bigger when foreign trade increases the variety choice available to consumers and producers, because variety choice is a source of increasing returns to scale. On the production side, a larger variety choice of intermediate inputs raises total factor productivity, and more intermediate inputs become available in larger sectors. On the demand side, a larger assortment of brands of a differentiated product raises the utility from spending a fixed amount of money on the product's consumption. Furthermore, Epifani and Gancia (2008) pointed out that under plausible parameter restrictions, scale economies could also affect the skill premium. To illustrate, they developed a model of monopolistic competition in which every country produced differentiated intermediate inputs with high-skilled and low-skilled workers in each of two sectors: a high-skill–intensive sector and a low-skill–intensive sector. On the demand side, the elasticity of substitution between the consumer goods produced by these sectors was assumed to be larger than 1. On the supply side, sector-specific intermediate inputs for the production of a final good were assumed to have a constant-elasticity-of-substitution production function.

The elasticity of substitution between the sector-specific intermediate inputs differed across sectors. In particular, the elasticity of substitution was assumed to be larger in the low-skill–intensive sector than in the high-skill–intensive sector; and both were assumed to be larger than the elasticity of substitution in consumption between the two final goods.[2] Epifani and Gancia also assumed that the intermediate goods were produced with increasing returns to scale due to fixed costs, the use of skilled and unskilled workers, and engagement in monopolistic competition by producers of intermediates.

Epifani and Gancia studied the impact on the skill premium of trade between two countries, one rich in high-skilled workers and the other rich in low-skilled workers. They identified two pertinent effects: a scale effect and a factor composition effect. The scale effect, which emanated from the fact that trade integration expands the size of the market, raised the wage of the skilled workers relative to the unskilled in each country. On the other hand, the composition effect affected the countries oppositely: It raised the skill premium in the country with the relatively larger endowment of high-skilled workers, and it reduced the skill premium in the country with the relatively larger endowment of low-skilled workers, via the familiar Stolper-Samuelson mechanism (see Chapter 2 for a discussion of this effect). Under these circumstances, the skill premium could rise in both countries when the scale effect was large in comparison to the Stolper-Samuelson effect.

However, the scale effect vanished when either the elasticity of substitution in consumption equaled 1 (constant expenditure shares) or the elasticity of substitution in production was the same in both sectors. Evidently, the assumed differences in the size of these elasticities were essential for the scale effect to drive the skill premium. And the scale effect was larger the better substitutes the consumption goods were for each other, the larger was the elasticity of substitution in production in the low-skill–intensive sector, and the smaller was the elasticity of substitution in production in the high-skill–intensive sector.

The critical roles of the elasticities of substitution in production stem from the fact that they affect the elasticity of output with respect to aggregate inputs used in an industry. In models of monopolistic competition of the type deployed by Epifani and Gancia (2008), there are two potential sources of economies of scale at the *industry* level. First, there are the economies of scale of individual firms engaged in the fabrication of intermediate inputs. An increase in the amount of resources available to an industry can induce an expansion of output per firm, which would reduce unit costs. Yet this mechanism was neutralized in their setup, where output per firm did not respond to the size of the sector. Second, there is the impact of the industry's size on the range of intermediate inputs available to producers; the larger the sector, the more intermediate inputs become available through market entry. Although more resources raise output proportionately for a given array of intermediate inputs, additional output is gained via an increase in total factor productivity with the rise in the number of intermediates. Moreover, this productivity effect is larger the less substitutable for each other are intermediate inputs in production. And this is indeed the source of the scale effects in Epifani and Gancia's model.

To justify the assumption that the elasticity of substitution of intermediate inputs is higher in lower-skill-intensive sectors, Epifani and Gancia (2008) examined evidence on the correlation between skill intensity and scale elasticities across sectors, where the scale elasticity reflects the percentage increase in a sector's output in response to a proportional increase in its employment of resources. In sectors with constant returns to scale, the scale elasticity equals 1, while in sectors with increasing returns to scale it exceeds 1. They found a positive correlation. That is, sectors that were more skill intensive exhibited larger economies of scale (see their figure 1).

Armed with this finding, Epifani and Gancia proceeded to examine the impact of market size expansion on the skill premium. Of particular interest are their estimates concerning two measures of the skill premium: first, the wage of nonproduction relative to production workers in manufacturing; and second, the returns to education, estimated from Mincerian wage equations (see Mincer 1974).[3] Using alternative measures of economic size—such as a country's GDP, its trade openness, and two synthetic measures that combined domestic size and the size of trade partners weighted by trade openness—they found that countries with greater economic growth experienced larger increases in their skill premia, measured by either Mincerian returns to education or by the relative wage of nonproduction workers.[4] These findings suggest that part of the rise in wage inequality was due to the expansion of market size, as a result of both domestic growth and globalization. Unfortunately, these estimates cannot be used to assess what fraction of the rise in inequality resulted from globalization through this channel.

FIRM HETEROGENEITY

Firm heterogeneity was introduced into trade theory in response to the discovery during the 1990s of new patterns in previously unavailable data sets. In these data, firms exhibited substantial heterogeneity within industries in productivity and size, and only a fraction of firms exported. Furthermore, exporters differed systematically from nonexporters, with exporters being larger and more productive. Bernard and Jensen (1995, 1999) discovered these patterns in US data, while subsequent studies confirmed them in other countries, including Canada, Colombia, France, Mexico, Morocco, Spain, and Taiwan (see Helpman 2011, chap. 5). Similar patterns were found for importing firms in more-recent studies. In the United States in 2007, only 35 percent of manufacturing firms exported, and only 20 percent imported. In that same year, exporters and importers employed more than twice as many workers as other firms did; their value added was higher by 21 percent and 32 percent, respectively; they paid higher wages; and they employed workers with higher skills (see tables 3 and 4 in Bernard, Jensen, Redding, and Schott 2016).

Melitz (2003) invented the canonical model for explaining these export patterns, and similar ideas were used to explain the import patterns.[5] In Melitz's model, labor is homogeneous and entrepreneurs pay an upfront "entry" cost to acquire a fabrication technology. The entry cost may consist of R&D expenditures for product design, or the expense of developing a suitable production technology, or outlays associated with forming a business enterprise. Importantly, however, the productivity of this enterprise is uncertain at the entry stage. At that stage, only the *statistical distribution* of productivity is known to the entrepreneur, and she learns her productivity *level* after the entry cost is sunk.

A company's business strategy is formed after entry, when the productivity of the technology becomes familiar. At that stage, staying in business entails fixed operating costs, such as the rental cost of offices and the cost of essential personnel, that do not depend on the scale of production. Accordingly, only firms with a high enough productivity level are profitable, while lower-productivity firms are not. In particular, there is a productivity cutoff such that all firms with lower productivity cut their losses by closing shop. Companies that stay in business serve the domestic market, but they may also choose to export. However, exporting entails a fixed cost of maintaining a beachhead in every destination country. For this reason, only firms with high enough productivity levels can profitably export, while the best export strategy of the other firms would not generate enough operating profits to cover the fixed export costs. Therefore, a cutoff productivity level exists such that only firms with higher productivity find it profitable to export. When the export cutoff exceeds the domestic cutoff, selection into exporting generates a sectoral structure that has the following features: Low-productivity firms, below the export cutoff, serve only the domestic market; while higher-productivity firms serve the domestic market and sell a fraction of their output to foreigners. In sum, not all entrants stay in the industry; and among those who do, the more-productive entrants export while the less-productive entrants serve only the domestic market. This makeup replicates the main patterns in the data, where exporters are larger and more productive than nonexporting firms.

In this model, trade liberalization raises the profitability of exporting, which induces exporters to expand output and foreign sales and motivates somewhat less-productive firms close to the export cutoff to start exporting. The export cutoff declines, and exporters raise their demand for domestic inputs. Since exporters compete with domestic firms for local resources, the cost of domestic inputs rises, thereby reducing the profitability of nonexporting firms. This decline in profitability pushes the least-productive firms—who were at the margin of profitability—into the red, and the domestic productivity cutoff rises. Consequently, the fraction of exporting firms increases. In addition, the industry's average productivity rises, due to both the exit of the least-productive firms and a shift in market share toward the exporters, who are more productive. The resulting productivity gains can be substantial. For example, following the formation of the Canada–US free trade agreement in 1989, Canadian labor productivity increased in the manufacturing sector by 4.1 percent due to the growth of exporters and by an additional 4.3 percent due to the contraction and exit of the least-productive plants in the industry (see table 2 in Melitz and Trefler 2012).[6]

In Melitz's original study, all workers were assumed to be identical, and all of them were paid the same wage independently of whether they were hired by high- or low-productivity firms, by exporters, or by nonexporters. For this reason, international trade affected the wage *level*, but not wage inequality. Nonetheless, by enriching that framework, subsequent studies combined firm heterogeneity with mechanisms that generate wage distributions in order to examine how wage inequality responds to globalization.

Using a one-sector model with monopolistic competition, Sampson (2014) explored the role of matching between heterogeneous firms and heterogeneous workers in shaping wage inequality. On the demand side, he assumed consumer preferences with a constant elasticity of substitution between brands of a differentiated product. On the business side, he adopted the Melitz (2003) assumptions: Entrants bore a fixed upfront cost; they faced uncertainty concerning the quality of their technologies; and once the nature of the technology became known, an entrepreneur decided whether to stay in the industry, and if she stayed, whether to export. Instead of assuming that all workers were alike, however, Sampson assumed that they differed in ability. Similarly to the assumption used with the matching models discussed in Chapter 6, he also assumed that the output level of a single variety was proportional to the number of manufacturing workers, where the factor of proportionality, that is, the productivity function, depended on the ability of the workers and the quality (productivity) of the technology. This productivity function was assumed to be log supermodular. As a result, there was positive assortative matching between workers and firms: More-productive firms hired more-able workers.

The range of technologies of incumbent firms was determined by the domestic cutoff, but the export cutoff and the resulting selection into exporting also played a role in shaping these firm–worker matches. The matching pattern determined in turn the distribution of wages. Since the productivity distribution of incumbents and their business strategies were endogenous, the distribution of wages was also endogenous and so was the resulting wage inequality. Similar to the matching discussed in Chapter 6, here too better matches were associated with higher inequality of earnings.

To understand the impact of trade on inequality in this economy, it is necessary to discover how globalization affects the productivity of the firms that remain in the industry. Sampson first considered a simplified world of symmetric countries with low fixed export costs that induce all incumbents to export. In this case, trade leads to an increase in the productivity level of the least-productive firms that remain in the industry, bringing about a rightward shift in the productivity distribution of incumbents (that is, making higher productivity levels more likely). He then showed that this shift in productivity leads to a *rematching* of workers and firms, which improves the matches of *all* workers. As a result, wage inequality rises throughout the entire distribution of earnings. Although the case in which all firms export is not realistic, it helps isolate a mechanism through which globalization raises wage inequality: the shift in the distribution of active technologies. The conclusion was that ". . . at sufficiently high levels of trade integration [that inspire all firms to export] wage inequality is always greater over all workers than in autarky" (Sampson 2014, p. 176).

When the fixed export cost is not low enough to induce all firms to export, there is an additional element that drives inequality: the discontinuity in labor demand by firms around the export productivity cutoff. This discontinuity arises because firms that do export at this productivity level have to be measurably larger than those who do not in order to cover the fixed export cost. Although Sampson was not able to derive analytical results for this case, he used simulations to corroborate the intuition that under these circumstances globalization has more-nuanced effects on inequality.

First, Sampson found that trade raised inequality among workers employed by exporters, that is, workers in the upper tail of the wage distribution. Second, it raised inequality at the lower end of the wage distribution when the productivity level of the least-productive incumbents increased. However, trade could sometimes *reduce* the productivity level of the least-productive incumbents, in which case trade integration would *reduce* inequality among the low-ability workers. Third, inequality increased when variable trade costs declined, but it followed an inverted U-shape as the fixed cost of exporting declined. That is, inequality increased initially and declined eventually.[7]

The inverted U-shape results from the fact that the distributions of wages are comparable when the economy does not export and when all firms export. But in between, when only a fraction of the firms export, exporting widens the wage gap between highly productive exporters and less-productive firms that serve only the domestic market. As a result, trade with selection into exporting by a fraction of the incumbents leads to more inequality than either autarky or a world where all firms export.

QUANTIFICATION

Although there are no estimates of how much globalization contributed to inequality through Sampson's (2014) mechanism, Burstein and Vogel (2017) used counterfactual analysis to study the impact of trade on inequality in a quantitative model in which both firm characteristics and worker attributes varied. Workers were aggregated into two categories: low-skilled and high-skilled. The number of products was exogenous; and producers of intermediate inputs, who varied in productivity, engaged in Bertrand competition, as in Bernard, Eaton, Jensen, and Kortum (2003).[8] Although Burstein and Vogel allowed average factor intensities to vary across sectors, in their design, producers of intermediate inputs that operated in the same industry but differed in productivity levels also differed in factor intensities (see their equations (3) and (13) and the discussion that follows the latter). Under their parameter restrictions, higher-productivity firms within an industry employed more high-skilled relative to low-skilled workers. Indeed, a positive correlation between firm productivity (or size) and the relative use of skilled workers was documented for the United States by Bernard, Jensen, Redding, and Schott (2016), for Mexico by Verhoogen (2008), for Argentina by Bustos (2011b), and for Chile by Harrigan and Reshef (2015).

In combination with selection into exporting as a result of the Bertrand competition, the higher skill intensity in more-productive firms generated an increase in the relative demand for skilled workers within sectors in response to trade liberalization. Under these circumstances, globalization could raise the relative employment of skilled workers within industries even when it raised the skill premium. For this reason, globalization could lead to a pervasive rise in the skill premium, and therefore in wage inequality, in both developed and developing countries. Although the Stolper-Samuelson mechanism magnifies the rise in the skill premium in rich countries and moderates it in poor countries, in the Burstein and Vogel framework wage inequality could rise in all countries. The question, however, was whether this theoretical possibility could generate quantitatively measurable results.

Burstein and Vogel's (2017) model of international trade consists of sixty countries and a region that encompasses the remaining parts of the world's economy, a large number of traded sectors, and service sectors that do not engage in foreign trade. As explained above, within sectors firms are assumed to be heterogeneous and higher-productivity firms employ more high-skilled relative to low-skilled workers. They calibrated the model to data from 2005 through 2007.

Holding endowments and technologies constant, they used it to carry out counterfactual experiments. In one experiment, trade costs were increased so as to drive all countries to autarky. The differences between autarky and the 2005 through 2007 outcomes provided estimates of the impact of globalization.

Importantly, in this counterfactual experiment both skilled and unskilled workers gained from trade; that is, moving from autarky to trade raised the *real* wages of both types of labor around the globe. Moreover, in all countries, with the exception of Russia, trade raised the wages of skilled workers proportionately more than the wages of unskilled workers. As a result, the skill premium, measured as the ratio of skilled wages relative to unskilled wages, increased in almost all countries (see their figure 2). This means that the Stolper-Samuelson effects were overwhelmed by the within-industry reallocations, including selection into exporting. Nonetheless, the rise of the skill premium varied across countries, being larger in more-open economies and in net exporters of skill-intensive products. The rise in the skill premium was largest in Lithuania, amounting to 12 percent, compared to an average of 5.1 percent. The skill premium rose by 2 percent in the United States and by 0.5 percent in Brazil.

Comparing the change in the skill premia as a result of moving from 1975 through 1977 to autarky and of moving from 2005 through 2007 to autarky, and using the difference between these two as an estimate of the model-based rise in the skill premium from 1975 through 1977 to 2005 through 2007, also showed a pervasive rise in the skill premium. The Philippines experienced the largest rise, and this was a little more than half the rise in Lithuania's skill premium from autarky to 2005 through 2007. This and the previous quantitative analysis suggest that the combined contribution to the rise of wage inequality of within-sectoral heterogeneity, selection into exporting, and factor proportions is potentially significant, yet modest.

A similar conclusion arises from Burstein and Vogel's (2017) analysis of a China shock. They examined the impact of an increase in

China's total factor productivity that would have raised its share of world output from 8 percent (China's share in 2006) to 20 percent, an exceptionally large change. And they found that in their model, China's expansion increased the skill premium in fifty-five out of the fifty-nine countries in their sample, but only by minuscule amounts under the assumption of free factor mobility across sectors. Under the alternative assumption of limited factor mobility, which was supposed to represent short-run effects, the skill premia increased by about three times as much, but remained small nevertheless (see their figure 6).

GROWTH

Sorting and matching in economies with heterogeneous workers and firms have also been used to study the impact of globalization on growth and inequality. The main idea is that both growth and inequality respond to trade exposure, and therefore both are endogenous in the long run. This view, developed in Grossman and Helpman (2018), contrasts with the alternative views that either inequality influences growth or that growth influences inequality (see Helpman 2004, chap. 6). This is not to deny that during the transition to a long-run growth trajectory, current inequality can temporarily affect future growth or that current growth can temporarily affect future inequality; the argument is instead that eventually growth and inequality are jointly determined by fundamental characteristics of the world economy. These characteristics include innovation technologies, specialized resources used by these technologies, the ability to convert research and development experience into usable knowledge, and the features of the international trade regime.

In Grossman and Helpman's framework, individuals differ by ability; and they can be employed either in manufacturing or in innovation, that is, they can be idea users or idea producers. In manufacturing, workers are matched with heterogeneous firms that produce varieties of intermediate inputs, and these firms engage in monopolistic competition. The intermediate inputs produce final consumer goods. In the idea-creating sector, workers are matched with heterogeneous research labs that generate ideas for new types of intermediate inputs. An entrepreneur in the manufacturing sector purchases the services of innovators to develop a new type of intermediate input, but the productivity of the technology to manufacture this input is learned only after the cost of R&D services has been sunk. An entrepreneur in the innovating sector rents a lab for her research projects, and the productivity of the lab becomes known only after the cost of the lab has been sunk. In other words, entrepreneurs in both sectors face risky investments. The range of intermediate inputs available for manufacturing evolves over time as new varieties are developed.

The functioning of the manufacturing sector is similar to that described by Sampson (2014), except that there are no fixed costs of either operating or exporting. For that reason, every firm that has a technology for a specialized intermediate input remains active, and it exports to other countries when trade is enabled. In the innovation sector, the number of new intermediate inputs created by a lab depends on the productivity of the lab, the ability of the workers employed by the lab, the number of these workers, and—as discussed in Romer (1990) and Grossman and Helpman (1991a,b)—the stock of useful knowledge available to the country. The stock of useful knowledge evolves over time according to the country's cumulative innovation experience, and possibly according to the cumulative innovation experience of its trade partners in a trading regime. The degree to which a country benefits from R&D investment in other countries varies across trade partners, and the pattern of these spillovers is assumed to be exogenous.[9]

The productivity functions of manufacturing technologies and research labs are assumed to be log supermodular, exhibiting complementarity between workers' abilities and employers' productivity or sophistication levels. As a result, there is positive assortative matching between workers and employers within both the manufacturing sector and the innovation sector. Grossman and Helpman also assumed that for every pair of workers, the higher-ability worker has a comparative advantage in innovation. Under these circumstances, workers with abilities above a threshold sort into innovation and workers with abilities below this threshold sort into manufacturing. This threshold is endogenous, however, and it plays a key role in the relationship between growth and inequality. A lower threshold implies that more workers are employed in innovation, leading to faster growth. And it also implies that matches improve for all workers, independently of where they are employed, thereby leading to a pervasive rise in wage inequality. These relationships between the threshold, the growth rate, and wage inequality are key for understanding the results that follow.

Grossman and Helpman (2018) studied economies with and without international R&D spillovers and economies with and without international capital mobility in the form of borrowing and lending. In the presence of international R&D spillovers, they found that the long-run outcomes did not depend on capital mobility. For this case, there were a number of main findings. First, globalization accelerated growth in all countries and brought about convergence of growth rates, in line with the endogenous growth results in Grossman and Helpman (1991b). When countries benefited from R&D spillovers from trade partners, their stocks of useful knowledge rose and their innovation costs fell. As a consequence, the ability thresholds above which workers sorted into innovation declined, leading to faster growth and more wage inequality in every country. That is, globalization *raised* both growth and inequality. Second, in a globalized world, an increase in R&D spillovers between any pair of countries accelerated growth in the entire world economy and raised wage inequality everywhere. Third, in a globalized world, an increase in any country's R&D subsidy raised its wage inequality relative to the other countries and brought about faster growth everywhere. These results underline the high degree of interdependence between countries in a global economy. Globalization leads not only to trade interdependence but also to interdependence in growth and inequality.

In the absence of international R&D spillovers, a country's stock of useful knowledge is determined by its own cumulative experience in R&D and the efficiency with which it converts this experience into useful knowledge. Under these circumstances, long-run outcomes depend on whether international capital flows are possible. In a global economy that traded only in goods, Grossman and Helpman found that the country that grew *fastest* in autarky grew at its autarky rate and had the same inequality as in autarky. In other words, this country's long-run growth and inequality were not affected by international trade. Nonetheless, the outcomes were different for the other countries. They grew faster in the globalized world than in autarky, but had the same inequality as in autarky. At the same time, their rates of innovation were the same as in autarky. These countries could benefit from faster growth without modifying their rates of innovation by piggybacking on the rate of innovation of the fastest-innovating country in the world. Trade enabled them to import intermediate inputs that were invented by the fastest-innovating country and thereby raise their own TFP growth rates.

Finally, in a world with no international R&D spillovers that trades in goods and enables international capital flows, Grossman and Helpman found that, as before, the country that innovated fastest in autarky experienced the same rate of growth and inequality as in autarky. But in this regime, all the other countries grew faster than in autarky yet had *lower* inequality than in autarky.

In this framework, globalization accelerates growth. This conclusion applies to globalization that entails international R&D spillovers and complete integration of goods and capital markets, as well as partial globalization with integration of goods markets only. If there are international R&D spillovers, globalization raises inequality in all countries. But in the absence of such spillovers, it does not affect inequality when only goods markets integrate, and it reduces inequality when both goods and capital markets integrate. These are theoretical findings, however, with no commensurate empirical evidence yet available.

9

Technology Choice

CHAPTER 8 described the impact of globalization on wage inequality when heterogeneous workers were matched with heterogeneous firms, and firms discovered the productivity of their technologies after investing in product development. The nature of these matches determined the slope of the wage function and thereby inequality. In this setting, foreign trade modified inequality by affecting the sorting of workers into different activities and the distribution of technologies in those activities, thereby motivating rematching between workers and firms. Nonetheless, a firm could not invest in order to draw a better technology or to improve the set of technologies available to it.

In Chapter 9, I first discuss wage inequality that arises when workers are heterogeneous and firms can choose among technologies of varying quality. These technology choices provide flexibility, enabling entrepreneurs and business firms to make joint decisions about technologies and the types of workers that will operate them. In addition, I discuss economic environments in which the nature of technical change is selected by business firms and directed to complement specific factors of production. This is especially important for understanding how globalization changes the incentives of inventors to target particular forms of innovation, because it provides a mechanism through which globalization can affect wages by triggering technical change. Under the circumstances, it is difficult to identify what part of wage inequality is caused by technology and what part by trade.[1]

SELECTING WORKERS AND TECHNOLOGIES

An early analysis of the joint choice of technology and worker abilities was developed by Yeaple (2005). In his model, workers varied by ability. A traditional sector supplied a homogeneous good in which there was no technology choice, and labor productivity increased with worker ability. In contrast, two technologies were available in the advanced sector that supplied varieties of a differentiated product, and labor productivity was higher for higher-ability workers operating either one of these technologies. One of the technologies surpassed the other in terms of labor productivity at all ability levels, but the better technology required higher fixed costs of operation. A firm that entered the advanced industry to produce a brand of the differentiated product could choose one technology or the other. Finally, higher-ability workers were assumed to have a *comparative advantage* in the advanced sector, and within this sector they had a comparative advantage operating the better technology.

Depending on the distribution of worker skills and features of the technologies, both technologies could survive the competitive pressure in the advanced sector, or only one of them might survive. The main analysis proceeded under the assumption that both technologies were used, which is also assumed below.

In Yeaple's framework, the least-able workers sorted into the traditional sector; the most-able workers sorted into the advanced sector in order to operate the better technology; and workers with midrange abilities sorted into the advanced sector in order to operate the inferior technology. Under these circumstances, wage inequality at the upper end of the distribution was determined by the labor productivity of workers using the better technology; wage inequality at the lower end of the distribution was determined by the labor productivity of workers using the traditional-sector technology; and in the middle range, wage inequality was determined by labor productivity of workers using the inferior technology in the differentiated product sector. Inequality across these groups depended in turn on the comparative advantage of workers across the three technologies.

When two symmetric countries traded with each other and there were fixed and variable trade costs, no trade occurred in traditional goods. With low enough fixed export costs, however, differentiated products were traded; and if both technologies were employed, all firms that invested in the better technology exported. Although there existed circumstances in which all firms—independently of their technology—exported, the interesting case arose when not all of them did: namely, when there was selection into exporting. In this case, a suitable restriction on fixed costs generated a dichotomous outcome: Firms that adopted the poorer technology served only the domestic market, while firms that adopted the advanced technology also exported. In sum, the exporters employed a better technology and hired more-able workers than did nonexporters.

Yeaple showed that in this framework, a reduction in variable trade costs prompts more firms to adopt the better technology in the differentiated product sector. The most-able workers among those who operated the inferior technology switch employment to firms operating the better technology, and the least-able workers among those who operated the inferior technology switch employment to the traditional sector. Moreover, relative wage changes conform to changes in employment: They rise for high-ability workers operating the advanced technology, decline for middle-ability workers operating the inferior technology, and do not change for workers manufacturing traditional goods. In addition, wages rise for workers who switch from the inferior to the superior technology and decline for workers who switch from the inferior technology in the differentiated product sector to the traditional sector.

These responses to globalization display wage and employment polarization, which is sometimes referred to as the "hollowing out of the middle class." Namely, the most-able and the least-able workers do better than workers with middle ability levels. Since labor market polarization of this type has been documented in the United States and sixteen European countries (see Goos, Manning, and Salomons 2009 and Autor 2014), one would hope that this analysis has identified a credible mechanism with substantial explanatory sway. Unfortunately, however, there is no reliable evidence to support the claim that globalization has played a big role in polarizing the labor market.

Sampson (2014) extended this analysis, allowing for a continuous distribution of worker abilities and a continuum of technology choices but no traditional sector. Better technologies were more expensive, and log supermodularity of the productivity function resulted in positive assortative matching between workers and firms. Since the choice of technology was endogenous, worker heterogeneity ensured heterogeneity of firms in as much as it proved equally profitable to bear the cost of a high- or low-productivity technology. Exporting entailed fixed costs, giving rise to selection into exporting. Exporters were more productive than were nonexporters, and they employed higher-ability workers. Sampson showed that in a world of symmetric countries, a decline in variable trade costs motivated some lower-productivity firms to become exporters and some of the highest-ability workers who were employed by nonexporters to switch employment to exporting firms. Although inequality of wages did not change among workers employed by companies that exported both before and after the trade shock, nor among workers who were employed by nonexporters before and after the trade shock, inequality increased among the workers who switched employment from nonexporting to exporting enterprises, and the wage gap between workers employed by exporters and nonexporters widened. No polarization arose in this case, however, because in the absence of a traditional sector the lowest productivity cutoff in the differentiated product sector was the same with or without foreign trade.

Similarly to Yeaple (2005), Bustos (2011b) also assumed that firms in the differentiated product industry could adopt one of two technologies: a high-fixed-cost technology, which was efficient (that is, cost effective) at large volumes of output, or a low-fixed-cost technology that was efficient at low volumes of output. Unlike Yeaple, however, Bustos had no homogeneous sector. In addition, she assumed that there were only two types of workers, high-ability skilled workers and low-ability unskilled workers; that both types of workers were essential in production; and that the technologies differed in factor intensities: The large-scale–efficient technology used a larger number of more-skilled relative to lower-skilled workers.

These features were combined with firm heterogeneity. Every entrant to the industry was randomly assigned a firm-specific productivity level that determined its variable production costs. Higher-productivity firms gained the same variable cost advantage in both technologies. As a result, higher-productivity firms had a comparative advantage in the use of the large-scale–efficient technology. Naturally, whether a firm chose to use this technology depended on how productive the firm was and on how large the skill premium was. An exceedingly high wage of skilled workers relative to the unskilled could make the variable cost of production with the large-scale–efficient technology so high as to offset its advantage over the small-scale–efficient technology at high output levels. When the skill premium was not too high, both technologies were used by incumbents, and high-productivity firms adopted the large-scale–efficient technology.

Fixed operating costs led to the exit of low-productivity firms, while fixed export costs led to the selection of the most-productive firms into exporting. For these reasons, some firms exited the industry after entry; the least-productive incumbents served only the domestic market and adopted the small-scale–efficient technology;

while the remaining incumbents exported. Among the exporters, the lower-productivity companies adopted the small-scale–efficient technology, while the higher-productivity companies adopted the large-scale–efficient technology.

In this model, a reduction in variable trade costs led some of the least-productive firms to exit the industry, and it led some exporters who initially used the small-scale–efficient technology to switch to the large-scale–efficient technology. It also led some of the nonexporting enterprises at the upper end of the nonexporters' productivity distribution to start exporting, with the most successful among them adopting the large-scale–efficient technology. Evidently, these within-industry reallocations raised the relative demand for skilled workers, both because a larger fraction of firms adopted the large-scale–efficient technology and because market shares were reallocated from enterprises that used the low-skill–intensive technology to enterprises that used the high-skill–intensive technology. As a result, the skill premium increased.

Bustos used this framework to study the impact of MERCOSUR—the free-trade area established in 1991 between Argentina, Brazil, Paraguay, Uruguay, and Venezuela—on Argentinian firms.[2] Brazilian tariff cuts were used to assess the response of the share of skilled workers in the employment of Argentinian firms (Brazil was Argentina's largest trade partner). These tariff cuts varied across sectors and differentially affected companies in different industries. Among firms above the median size, 76 percent exported; while among firms below the median size, only 38 percent of firms exported. Bustos's estimates suggest that the average reduction of the tariffs, which amounted to 23 percent, brought about an 8 percent reduction in the share of skilled workers in companies below the median size and an increase of 6 percent in the share of skilled workers in firms above the median. These figures represent a significant shift in labor composition across firms. The skill composition was affected both among production and nonproduction workers, with the strongest effect on the share of skilled workers among nonproduction workers taking place within firms at the top quartile of the size distribution. Unfortunately, this study provides no evidence concerning the impact of MERCOSUR on the skill premium.

DIRECTED TECHNICAL CHANGE

The previous section, "Selecting Workers and Technologies," discussed how every firm advanced its business prospects by selecting a technology from an available array. But the assortment of these technologies was fixed. For this reason, globalization influenced the technology choices without modifying the set of accessible technologies. In contrast, Wood (1994) argued that foreign trade influenced the direction of technical change and that disregarding this effect biased downward estimates of the impact of trade on the composition of labor demand.[3] After discussing traditional estimates, he stated:

> Neither the conventional nor the modified FCT [factor content of trade] method allows for the effects of trade on technical progress: the former takes factor input coefficients as given; the latter takes production function parameters as given. This omission is of limited significance in the South, which is usually a taker rather than a maker of new technologies. . . . In the North, by contrast, the exclusion of trade-induced technical change probably has a large effect on the accuracy of the demand impact estimates. Most Northern manufacturers of labor-intensive goods seem to have reacted to Southern competition by seeking new production techniques that use less unskilled labor (p. 159).

Wood speculated that allowing for defensive innovation would double his estimates of the impact of trade on the skill composition of labor demand (p. 11). Yet despite his view that endogenous technical change was important, he did not know how to incorporate it into the analysis.

Years later, Acemoglu (2003) developed a theoretical framework for investigating the effect of foreign trade on the direction of technical change. To this end, he incorporated growth based on quality ladders into a two-sector factor proportions trade model with low-skilled and high-skilled workers.[4] In one sector, intermediate (or capital) goods were produced with low-skilled workers; in the other, intermediate goods were produced with high-skilled workers; and in each sector, the intermediates were combined with labor to fabricate a final consumer good. This structure sharply identified one sector as being low-skill–intensive and the other as being high-skill–intensive. Further, in every sector innovators could target specific intermediates for quality improvements. The size of a successful quality jump was constant, but the probability of success was larger the more resources were invested in innovation. Because every sector used a continuum of intermediates, these innovation efforts improved the quality of a fraction of the intermediates, thereby raising the sector's total factor productivity (TFP). The more the sector invested in innovation, the larger was the fraction of intermediates that were successfully improved; and therefore, the faster was the sector's TFP growth. By assumption, intermediates were not traded internationally and globalization entailed trade in final goods only.

In this model only one country, the United States, engaged in innovation; and private incentives governed the direction and extent of technical change, that is, the extent to which inventors targeted the low-skill– or high-skill–intensive sector. A quality improvement, in the form of a climb to a higher rung on the quality ladder, gave the innovator monopoly power until her quality was surpassed; and the operating profits derived from this monopoly power provided incentives to invest in R&D. Intellectual property (IP) rights to these profits were secured in the United States but not necessarily in the other countries, which were viewed as being less developed. Yet the less-developed countries could adopt the best available technologies, albeit they could not implement them as efficiently as could the US manufacturers.

Significantly, in this framework the direction of technical change, which was reflected in the long-run sectoral differences in TFP levels, was determined by two major forces. One was the price effect. A higher price of a consumer good made it more profitable to improve intermediate products for the production of this good, which raised the rate of R&D investment in these intermediates and consequently raised the industry's productivity level. The second force was the market size effect. The more workers used a technology, the higher were the profits from improving an intermediate product designed for these workers, which raised the rate of R&D investment in these intermediates and consequently raised the industry's productivity level. But this meant that in a closed economy—when the United States did not trade with the less-developed countries—the relative supply of skilled workers in the United States had conflicting effects on the direction of technical change. On the one hand, the relatively greater availability of skilled workers raised the relative supply of skill-intensive products, which reduced their relative price; and this encouraged relatively more innovation in the *low*-skill–intensive sector. On the other hand, the relatively greater availability of skilled workers raised the market size for skill-intensive innovations, which encouraged relatively more innovation in the *high*-skill–intensive sector. The resolution of these conflicting pressures on sectoral relative productivity levels depended on the elasticity of substitution between high-skill–intensive and low-skill–intensive products in consumption, which determined in turn the elasticity of substitution between high-skilled and low-skilled workers in overall manufacturing.

When the countries traded with each other, the price effects depended on the *effective* relative supplies (that is, factor quantities adjusted for country-specific efficacies in the use of frontier-quality intermediates) of low-skilled and high-skilled workers in the *world* economy; while the market size effects depended on the relative supplies of low-skilled and high-skilled workers in the innovating country, the United States.[5] Acemoglu then showed that—under some plausible parameter restrictions—international trade led the relatively skill-rich US economy to bias technical change toward the skill-intensive sector. In consequence, globalization raised the US skill premium, and this rise was larger than it would have been in the absence of innovation. Using the factor content estimates from Borjas, Freeman, and Katz (1997), Acemoglu (2003, p. 220) calculated that his model could explain about one-fifth of the de facto rise in the US skill premium between 1980 and 1995. Although explaining one-fifth of the change in the data is significant but not overwhelming, without trade-induced technical change the model would have produced a rise in the skill premium that was half as large, amounting to about one-tenth of the actual increase. In conclusion, this exercise suggests that although the indirect effect of foreign trade on the skill premium through induced technical change might be comparable in size to the direct effect, their combined impact was modest overall.

Offshoring can also instigate directed technical change, which raises the question of whether it can generate large overall effects on inequality. Acemoglu, Gancia, and Zilibotti (2015) investigated this question by constructing an analytical model of two countries, one with an endowment of low-skilled and high-skilled workers, the other (for convenience) with an endowment of low-skilled workers only. They called the former country West and the latter East, but it is equally plausible to call the former North and the latter South or the former developed and the latter less-developed. Clearly, in this case the former country was relatively rich in skilled labor.

Similarly to Acemoglu (2003), a low-skill–intensive product was produced with specialized intermediate inputs (or tasks), and these inputs were produced by low-skilled workers. Likewise, a high-skill–intensive product was produced with specialized intermediate inputs (or tasks), but these inputs were produced by high-skilled workers. The low-skill–intensive and high-skill–intensive products were then combined, under the assumption of a constant-elasticity-of-substitution production function, to fabricate a final consumer good.

Unlike Acemoglu (2003), however, where innovators improved a fixed assortment of intermediate inputs, Acemoglu, Gancia, and Zilibotti (2015) assumed that R&D was directed toward inventing new specialized intermediates for one sector or the other. As more intermediates became available in a sector, its labor productivity increased. In other words, this study replaced productivity-enhancing inventions on a quality ladder with a productivity-enhancing expansion of intermediate inputs.[6] Intermediate inputs were invented at a cost in the skill-rich country, and patents protected the property rights of the inventors, who collected monopoly rents that provided the incentive to innovate. But every inventor had to decide whether to invest in the invention of an intermediate that was suitable for low-skilled or high-skilled workers. This led to directed technical change.

All intermediates could be produced in the skill-rich country. But, as in Grossman and Rossi-Hansberg (2008), the production of low-skill intermediates could also be offshored to the skill-poor country. Offshoring entailed a fixed and a variable cost, however. Since the wage rate of low-skilled workers was lower (by construction) in the skill-poor country, offshoring traded off lower manufacturing costs against the fixed and variable offshoring costs.[7] Under these circumstances, the scale of offshoring was a choice variable, part of the inventor's (or the technology buyer's) business strategy. As a result, whether technical change was directed toward low-skill or high-skill intermediate inputs depended on the cost of offshoring. As in Acemoglu (2003), there was a price effect and a market size effect, except that the latter also depended on the magnitude of offshoring.

Acemoglu, Gancia, and Zilibotti (2015) showed that for an exogenous level of offshoring and constant technology levels (that is, an unvarying range of intermediate inputs available in every sector), an increase in offshoring increased the real wage of low-skilled workers in the skill-poor country, increased the real wage of high-skilled workers in the skill-rich country, and raised the skill premium in the skill-rich country, but it could increase or reduce the real wage of low-skilled workers in the skill-rich country.[8]

These effects, which were derived under the assumption of unchanging technologies, identified several important relationships. More offshoring entailed relocating the production of low-skill intermediates from the skill-rich to the skill-poor country, where the wage was lower. This relocation reduced the average cost of low-skill intermediates and thereby the relative price of the goods produced with them. As a result, the demand for the low-skill–intensive goods increased and with it increased the demand for labor in the skill-poor country, which in turn raised the wage rate of its (low-skilled) workers. In the skill-rich country, the relocation of low-skill intermediates reduced the *relative* demand for low-skilled workers, which raised the skill premium and the real wage of the skilled workers. But the unskilled workers in the skill-rich country faced two opposing influences on their demand *level*. On the one hand, the demand for their services declined as fewer low-skill intermediates were produced in that country. On the other hand, the demand for their services increased in response to the surge in demand for low-skill–intensive products as a result of the fall in their price. For this reason, the low-skilled wage could rise or fall in the skill-rich country.

When both offshoring and technical change were allowed to respond to market conditions, Acemoglu, Gancia, and Zilibotti showed that (under some parameter restrictions) a reduction in the fixed cost of offshoring increased the scale of offshoring. But it induced high-skill–biased technical change for initially high offshoring costs and low-skill–biased technical change for initially low offshoring costs, where the skill-bias of the technology was measured by the ratio of the sectoral productivity levels. In other words, the relationship between the fixed cost of offshoring and the skill-bias of technology had an inverted U-shape. This inverted U-shape arose because the price effect dominated the incentives to innovate when the offshoring costs were high, and the market size effect held sway when the costs of offshoring were low. Importantly, however, independently of the response of the induced technical change, lower fixed costs of offshoring brought about faster growth. Lower fixed costs also reduced the gap between the wages of low-skilled workers in the two countries and raised the skill-premium in the skill-rich country when the elasticity of substitution between the intermediate inputs was large relative to the elasticity of substitution between the sectoral outputs (see their proposition 4).

Calibrating this model to data from the United States and China for the year 2000, and assuming that the United States was the skill-rich country, Acemoglu, Gancia, and Zilibotti (2015) examined a number of scenarios. First, they examined what the US skill premium would have been if the United States had been in autarky. In this and the subsequent exercises, the skill premium was defined as the ratio of the average wage of workers with some college education or more relative to the average wage of workers with a high school education or less. They found that instead of a skill premium of 1.9 in 2000, the autarky skill premium would have been 1.26. According to this quantification, foreign trade had a large impact on the skill premium, much larger than estimated by the other studies discussed so far. Moreover, 40 percent of the estimated rise in the skill premium was attributed to skill-biased technical change, which is comparable to the finding in Acemoglu (2003) about the impact of the direct and indirect effects of trade on the skill premium.

Second, Acemoglu, Gancia, and Ziliboti studied the impact of a fall in the fixed cost of offshoring. The size of this decline was calibrated to generate a 20 percent increase in the US volume of trade as a share of GDP, similar to the actual rise between 2000 and 2008. The cost of innovation was chosen to generate an annual 2 percent growth rate of income per capita, and the wage in China was selected to equal 16 percent of the US wage of low-skilled workers. This fall in the offshoring cost raised the US growth rate to 2.2 percent, a significant change. It also raised the skill premium from 1.9 to 2.06. Further, it raised the welfare level of all workers. Using the equivalent variation in consumption to measure these welfare changes, they found that Chinese workers gained the most, 26.4 percent (see their table 1); US low-skilled workers gained the least, 1.3 percent; while US high-skilled workers gained 8 percent.

These welfare gains emanated from the acceleration of growth. To neutralize the growth effect and focus the analysis purely on off-shoring, Acemoglu, Gancia, and Zilibotti carried out a calculation in which the fall in the offshoring cost discussed above was combined with an increase in the cost of innovation that jointly left the US growth rate at 2 percent. Under this scenario, Chinese workers still gained the most in welfare terms, 20.8 percent. But US low-skilled workers suffered a welfare loss of 3.1 percent, and US high-skilled workers enjoyed a welfare gain of 3.3 percent. The skill premium went up as before to 2.06 (see their table 1).

All the above-discussed estimates have to be treated with caution. They do suggest, however, that the feedback from directed technical change can be a potent force through which globalization influences inequality. In this sense, Wood (1994) was right in emphasizing this channel. But it is also fair to conclude that although we now have a better theoretical understanding of this feedback, we do not yet have reliable estimates of its size.

10

Residual Inequality

LABOR MARKETS are subject to a variety of frictions that prevent instantaneous adjustment of employment and wages. Some of these frictions are designed by governments, such as minimum wages or firing costs; others are ingrained in a functioning economy, such as the cost of finding a job or the cost of switching jobs. The latter may arise in turn from costs of moving to a different location, a different industry, or a different occupation (see the discussion in Chapter 7). Additionally, in many countries labor unions play an essential role in wage determination, be this within firms, within industries, or at the country level.

Labor market frictions vary substantially across countries. Numerous studies that examined the influence of these frictions on foreign trade and wages have shed light on wage inequality (see Helpman 2011, chap. 5 for a review). A key implication of such frictions is that unemployment emerges as an intrinsic outcome. Moreover, they often endow business firms with leverage over labor compensation. Although different forms of labor market frictions operate through mechanisms that differ in details, they all lead to unemployment and often to varying wage outcomes. Yet despite the recognition of these frictions, a paucity of evidence exists concerning the size of their effects.

Skills play a noteworthy role in shaping individual earnings, notwithstanding the fact that luck matters, too. Yet skills are difficult to measure, and they depend on a host of personal characteristics such as ability, talent, schooling, experience, and the like. Since the work of Mincer (1974), however, three observable characteristics—education, experience, and gender—have been used to explain differences in wages across individuals. As successful as this approach has been, it accounts for only a fraction of the variation in wages. The residual fraction—which cannot be explained by these attributes—is referred to as "residual inequality" (see Katz and Murphy 1992). Residual inequality increased over time, and the sources of this increase are still debated.

After estimating a wage equation by regressing log wages on worker characteristics, the inequality of log wages can be decomposed into inequality due to observed attributes and inequality due to unobserved attributes. The latter component represents an empirical measure of residual inequality. Although different yardsticks of dispersion can be used, such as the 90/10 percentile wage ratio, the standard deviation of log wages, or the Theil index of the distribution of wages, the decomposition into an observed and an unobserved part provides indispensable information about the sources of inequality.

Katz and Murphy (1992) pointed out the contribution of residual inequality to the rise in the college wage premium in the 1980s in the United States. But their estimates were challenged by Lemieux (2006), who attributed this rise to an "episodic" event and to compositional changes. In response, Autor, Katz, and Kearney (2008) conducted a detailed analysis of the data, concluding that the rise in inequality was not episodic, and especially so in the upper tail of the wage distribution (the 90/50 percentile ratio), where inequality increased nearly steadily from 1980 to 2005. Further, although changes in the composition of the labor force exerted upward pressure on residual wage inequality from the late 1980s to 2005, inequality was concentrated in the lower tail of the wage distribution and ". . . changes in earning dispersion within narrowly defined demographic groups, remain a key force in the evolution of both upper- and lower-tail U.S. residual wage inequality" (p. 301). They found that between 1973 and 2005, the 90/10 percentile ratio of wages of males increased by 34.6 log points, of which 12.8 log points were attributed to residual inequality and about two-thirds of the latter resulted from the rise of the 90/50 percentile ratio.

Rising residual wage inequality played a large role in increasing wage dispersion in other countries too. In Sweden, for example, residual wage inequality accounted for 70 percent of wage dispersion in 2001 (measured as the standard deviation of log wages), and it contributed 87 percent to the rise in wage inequality between 2001 and 2007 (see table 3 in Akerman, Helpman, Itskhoki, Muendler, and Redding 2013). Likewise, residual wage inequality accounted for 59 percent of wage dispersion in 1994 in Brazil, where it also accounted for 49 percent of the rise in wage inequality between 1986 and 1995 (see Helpman, Itskhoki, Muendler, and Redding 2017). Evidently, the importance of residual wage inequality is not confined to rich countries.

A number of studies addressed the impact of globalization on residual wage inequality, emphasizing alternative mechanisms of wage determination. These mechanisms included labor market frictions in the form of fair wages (Egger and Kreickemeier 2009; Amiti and Davis 2012), efficiency wages (Davis and Harrigan 2011), and search and matching (Davidson, Matusz, and Shevchenko 2008; Helpman, Itskhoki, and Redding 2010; Helpman, Itskhoki, Muendler, and Redding 2017). Combined with firm heterogeneity, each of these mechanisms generates a wage distribution among workers with *similar* characteristics; because these models predict that within the same industry, firms with higher productivity pay higher wages to workers of the same types. The positive correlation between firm size and wages, known as the wage-size premium, has been a well-established feature of the data for a long time (see Oi and Idson 1999). By combining international trade with a wage-size premium mechanism, recent studies have shown that due to *selection into exporting*, exporting firms—which are larger and more productive than nonexporters— pay significantly higher wages. The relationship between exporting and wages then implies that trade affects wage gaps between similar workers employed by firms with different characteristics, as a result of which trade affects residual wage inequality. An analogous role is played by *selection into importing*.

FAIR WAGES

A model of fair wages was employed by Amiti and Davis (2012) to study the impact of trade liberalization during the 1990s on wage inequality in Indonesia. In their model, workers were all alike; but, due to fairness considerations, wages were an increasing function of profits. As a result, wages varied across firms according to the differences in their profit levels; and this variation—together with the distribution of employment across firms—generated a distribution of wages among similar workers. In this way, the model focused on residual inequality.

In the Amiti and Davis analytical framework, there were two types of firms. One type produced intermediate inputs with labor only, using a unit of labor per unit of output. These firms faced a constant unit cost and engaged in competitive pricing. This resulted in zero profits, and therefore these manufacturers paid the lowest wage rate. A second type of firm supplied varieties of a differentiated product and engaged in monopolistic competition. After bearing an upfront entry cost, a producer of a brand of the differentiated product learned the productivity level of her technology as well as her idiosyncratic trade costs: the proportional cost of exporting the final good and the proportional cost of importing intermediate inputs. Her production technology required intermediate inputs and labor, and total factor productivity was higher the more types of intermediate inputs were engaged in production.

As in Melitz (2003), there was the same fixed cost of exporting to each and every country. In addition, there was a fixed cost of importing an intermediate input from a specific country. After entry, every manufacturer of a final good had to decide whether to stay in the industry, and if she stayed, whether to import intermediate inputs or to rely only on domestic intermediates, and whether to export the final product. The exporting and importing decisions were interrelated. An exporter had a bigger market for her product than a nonexporter, which made it more attractive to import intermediate inputs. But the profitability of exports depended on both the firm's productivity and on its trade costs. Other things being equal, a firm with low export costs might have chosen to export, in which case it found it more profitable to also import intermediates. Similarly, other things being equal, a firm with low import costs might have chosen to import intermediate inputs, which by lowering fabrication costs would make it more profitable to export. Since both exporting and importing entailed fixed costs, however, firms *selected* into exporting and importing.

In particular, the most-productive firms that were not too unlucky in their draws of trade costs engaged in both exporting and importing. And due to the fair-wage constraint, these firms paid the highest wages. On the other side were the least-productive firms that suffered from poor draws of trade costs; they did not import intermediate inputs, did not export their output, and paid low wages. Firms with particularly low productivity draws and draws of high trade costs were weeded out: They did not remain in the industry. Among the incumbents, there were also firms that served the home market only and imported intermediates, as well as firms that served the domestic market and exported their products but did not import intermediates.

In the Indonesian data studied by Amiti and Davis (2012), selection into importing and exporting followed the pattern predicted by the model. Only 5 percent of the firms imported inputs and exported a fraction of their output, 10 percent exported output but did not import inputs, and 14 percent imported inputs but did not export. Exporters were larger and more productive than were domestic firms, importers were larger and more productive than were exporters, and globally engaged firms that imported and exported were the largest and most productive. In addition, exporters paid 27.5 percent higher wages than did domestic firms, importers of intermediate inputs paid 46.8 percent higher wages, and globally engaged firms that both imported and exported paid 66.4 percent higher wages (see their table 1A). These wage premia declined to 7.6 percent, 14.6 percent, and 25.4 percent, respectively, after controlling for other features of the firms, such as their employment levels or sectoral affiliation. These data provided rich variation for examining the differential effects of tariff cuts on wages.

Cuts in tariffs on final goods had contrasting effects from cuts in tariffs on intermediate inputs. Reductions in output tariffs increased wages paid by exporters relative to nonexporters, raising wage dispersion within industries. In contrast, cuts in tariffs on intermediate inputs increased wages paid by importers relative to wages paid by nonimporting firms (see their table 2A). Since their data allowed them to estimate these effects only on average wages paid by the Indonesian firms, some of the observed wage responses might have been related to the rematching of different types of workers with firms, thereby reflecting changes in workforce composition. Although Amiti and Davis argued that these compositional effects were small, they remain a concern for evaluating the size of their estimates. In any case, Amiti and Davis did not report the impact of these tariff cuts on measures of overall inequality (such as the Theil index), which makes it impossible to form an opinion about whether the changes in inequality were small or large.

SEARCH AND MATCHING

Search and matching in labor markets, of the type developed by Mortensen and Pissarides (1994) and Diamond (1982a,b) for the study of macroeconomic determinants of unemployment, are a prime ingredient in recent studies of trade and wages. In this framework, firms post vacancies and unemployed workers search for jobs (in some studies, employed workers search for better jobs). Workers are matched with vacancies, but only some workers succeed in finding a job and only some vacancies are filled. The degree of success of the matching process depends on features of the labor market; in more-efficient markets, more matches are realized, and some markets favor workers, while others favor employers. Matched firms and workers engage in wage bargaining. Failure to reach an agreement is costly to both the workers and the firms, because it raises the number of unfilled vacancies for firms and some of the workers remain unemployed. As a result, every party has an incentive to reach an agreement. Understandably, wage bargaining takes place in the shadow of these costs, which consequently affect the wage agreements. International trade modifies the choices available to firms and the employment opportunities available to workers. Through changes in these options, trade modifies wages and employment.

Helpman, Itskhoki, and Redding (2010) developed a theory of trade and wages that combined a Melitz-style economy (2003) with search and matching. In this theory, firms pay an upfront entry cost and discover the productivity of their technology after this cost is sunk. Once they learn the quality of their technology, firms can choose to exit if their technologies are not profitable, they can stay and serve only the domestic market, or they can stay and serve the domestic as well as the foreign markets. If they choose to operate in the industry, they post vacancies for positions. Some of the unemployed workers who search for jobs are then matched with some of these vacancies.

Workers are identical ex ante, which means that before being hired every worker appears to be equally suitable for every position. But the productivity of a worker in a designated job is a random draw from a commonly known distribution, which equally applies to every job and every individual. In view of this uncertainty, firms screen workers who were matched with their vacancies, in order to improve the mix of their employees. The screening process is costly and imperfect, however. In particular, a firm can improve the average productivity of its workforce by ensuring that the fit of every employee to his position is above a selected threshold; yet it cannot assess the exact productivity of each worker. Firms differ in the productivity of their technology, which is their *core* productivity, and more-productive firms have a stronger incentive to engage in screening. As a result, firms with higher *core* productivity end up with higher *labor* productivity due both to their higher core productivity and due to the better fit of their workers to positions within the firms. A firm's optimal level of screening also depends on whether it chooses to serve only the domestic market or also to export, because larger sales make a larger investment in screening more profitable. Selection into exporting therefore provides firms with an additional incentive to screen their workers, which skews the distribution of labor productivity of incumbents in favor of exporters. This skewness plays an important role in the emergence of wage inequality within sectors.

Following matching and screening, every firm bargains over wages with its retained workers, that is, those who passed the screening test. Wage negotiations lead to higher wages being paid by more-productive firms.[1] Firms with higher core productivity are bigger in terms of employment and revenue, and the most productive among them select into exporting. As a result, exporters pay higher wages than nonexporters, in line with the evidence. An important implication of this theory is that ex-ante identical workers are paid different wages, giving rise to residual inequality. If workers differed in observable characteristics such as education, experience, or gender, then they would be compensated for these traits in addition to the pay they received for passing the screening assessments. Under these circumstances, wage inequality would reflect a combination of inequality due to variation in observable worker characteristics and residual inequality.

As in Melitz (2003), by making exports more profitable trade liberalization brings somewhat less-productive firms into the fold of exporters and forces some of the least-productive firms to close shop. Moreover, these reallocations affect wage inequality. Inequality rises in response to trade liberalization when the initial level of protection is high, and inequality declines when the initial level of protection is low. That is, trade liberalization has a nonmonotonic effect on wage inequality within sectors. This nonmonotonicity is related to the rise in the fraction of exporters in reaction to the decline of trade impediments. In autarky, no firm exports and all the variation in wages across firms is driven by the smooth variation across firms in core productivity levels and the smooth response in hiring and screening to this variation. When the trade impediments are so low that all firms export, the variation in wages is also smooth for similar reasons.

Not so for trade frictions in between, which generate selection into exporting. In this case, a smooth variation takes place within the group of domestically oriented manufacturers and within the group of exporters. But, as explained at the beginning of this chapter, close to the export cutoff there is a marked difference between the domestic firms and the exporters; the latter are discretely larger in terms of employment and revenue (this jump in activity is designed to compensate for the fixed cost of exporting). In addition, Helpman, Itskhoki, and Redding (2010) showed that around the export cutoff, exporters invest discretely more in screening and they pay discretely higher wages. These higher wages are supported by discretely higher average labor productivity that is achieved with the higher screening efforts. In other words, the slightly more productive firms that find it profitable to export pay discretely higher wages. This gap in wages generates additional wage inequality between exporters and nonexporters. As long as either of these groups of firms is small, inequality does not deviate much from the autarky level, and inequality peaks when the fraction of exporting firms is significant but not very large.

This model yields simple equations for the variation of wages, employment, and selection into exporting across firms within an industry. Helpman, Itskhoki, Muendler, and Redding (2017) extended this model to allow firms to differ not only along their core productivity dimension but also in their fixed cost of exporting and in their efficacy of screening. In this extended framework, an entrant into an industry draws a core productivity level, a fixed cost of exporting, and a screening efficacy level. Thus, every firm is characterized by three attributes. These additional sources of variation were justified by the need to give the model a chance to replicate features of the data. For example, although in typical data sets exporters are more likely to be more productive than are nonexporters, it is not the case that *every* exporter is more productive than *every* domestic firm. Allowing the fixed export costs to vary across firms permits some firms with high core productivity to have high fixed export costs and some lower core-productivity firms to have low fixed export costs. Under these circumstances, a firm with lower core productivity may find it profitable to export because it also faces a low fixed export cost, while a higher core-productivity firm may find it unprofitable to export because it faces a high fixed export cost.

Helpman, Itskhoki, Muendler, and Redding showed how this model can be estimated and how the resulting estimates can be used to portray the distribution of wages. Data on characteristics of individual workers and individual firms, and information about which workers are employed by each and every firm are needed for this purpose. Fortunately, rich data sets of this type are now available for

Table 10.1 Sources of Wage Inequality in Brazil (in percent)

	Worker Observables	Between-firm	Within-firm	Covariance
1994 level	13	39	37	11
1986–1995 change	2	86	−11	24

Variance decomposition of log wages.
Data source: Helpman, Itskhoki, Muendler, and Redding (2017, table 2).

a number of countries. Helpman, Itskhoki, Muendler, and Redding used a Brazilian episode to illustrate this methodology.

Brazil liberalized its economy over a number of years, culminating with a major trade liberalization in 1991 with the formation of the MERCOSUR free trade area (see the discussion of Bustos 2011b, in Chapter 9). Helpman, Itskhoki, Muendler, and Redding (2017) used formal-sector data for their analysis (Brazil also has a large informal sector), starting in 1986 and ending in 1998. Their main annual estimates used twelve manufacturing industries and five occupations, and information about approximately six million workers and more than 90,000 firms. They used Mincer wage equations to estimate a sector-occupation-specific wage component for every firm. The distribution of this component was then taken to represent the distribution of residual wages.

Table 10.1 shows the decomposition of the variance of log wages into its component parts that emerged from these estimates. The first row shows the decomposition of this variance for 1994, while the second row shows the decomposition of the change in this variance between 1986, prior to the trade liberalization, and 1995, subsequent to the trade liberalization. The first striking observation is that the share of worker observables in explaining wage inequality was small; it explained only 13 percent of the variance of log wages in 1994 and only 2 percent of the change in this variance between 1986 and 1995. The variation in the firm-specific component was the largest,

Table 10.2 Residual Wage Inequality in Brazil: 1994

	Employed by nonexporters	Employed by exporters
Model-based	0.42	0.42
Data-based	0.42	0.35

Standard deviation of residual log wages.
Data Source: Helpman, Itskhoki, Muendler, and Redding (2017, table 6).

explaining the lion's share of wage inequality both in 1994 and in the change between 1986 and 1995. In 1994, the between-firm variation accounted for 39 percent of the variance; and it accounted for 86 percent of the change in the variance between 1986 and 1995. It is apparent from these estimates that the firm-specific wage component played a major role in generating wage inequality during that period.

The estimates obtained by Helpman, Itskhoki, Muendler, and Redding were used to create a cross-worker distribution of wage portions that were not due to workers' observable characteristics. Those distributions were compared with the distributions of these same wage components in the data. Two model-based and data-based measures of dispersion of these distributions are presented in Table 10.2 for 1994. We see from this table that the model-based and data-based measures coincide for employees of nonexporting firms, but that the model overestimates the dispersion of these wage components among employees of exporting firms. This deviation is due to the fact that the fraction of exporting firms was small (less than 10 percent). On the other hand, the estimates precisely captured the export employment premium and the export wage premium, where the former reflects the extra employment chosen by exporters around the export cutoff, and the latter reflects the extra wages paid by exporters around the export cutoff (see their table 7).

Using the 1994 estimates, Helpman, Itskhoki, Muendler, and Redding simulated the impact of trade impediments on inequality. First, they found that reductions in trade impediments first raise inequality until it peaks, followed by declines in inequality in response to further declines in trade frictions, as predicted by the theoretical model. Second, they found that declines in variable trade costs lead to a higher peak of inequality than declines in fixed export costs. When disregarding the multiple destinations of different exporters, the former peak was 10.7 percent above autarky, while the latter was 7.6 percent above autarky. Allowing for multiple destinations raised the former peak to 23.3 percent above autarky and the latter to 19.0 percent (see their figures 1 and 3). Evidently, multiple export destinations, which feature in the data, amplify the effects of trade on residual wage inequality.

In conclusion, residual wage inequality is not only important in size, it is also considerably responsive to foreign trade conditions. For this reason an analysis of the effects of globalization on inequality is most likely incomplete if it disregards the impact of the trade environment on residual wage inequality.

Conclusion

THIS BOOK has taken the reader on a journey through an extensive literature devoted to exploring the relationship between globalization and inequality. Despite the large scale of the sources on which the book's narrative is built, it has left out many studies that are related to this topic. My decision to include some studies and exclude others was driven by two considerations: first, to produce a short and readable book that would be of interest to experts and nonexperts alike; and second, to cover all the major topics in a fair and balanced way. This means in particular that the collection of studies discussed in the book should be representative of the entire literature. As usual in these situations, judgment calls had to be made. Other experts might have chosen to report a somewhat different mix of research findings, or they might have emphasized different aspects of the relationship between globalization and earnings inequality. Be this as it may, I hope that my choices are sensible.

We have seen how the rise of the college wage premium during the 1980s prompted economists to study the role of foreign trade and foreign direct investment in shaping wage inequality. Although these early studies, carried out mostly during the 1990s, found that globalization contributed to the rise in wage inequality, they also concluded that this contribution was small. Moreover, they concluded that skill-biased technical change was most likely responsible for the changes in wage patterns that were seen in rich and poor countries alike. The research designs used in these studies relied heavily on the traditional approach to foreign trade and particularly on the factor proportions trade theory. The Stolper-Samuelson theorem took center stage in this endeavor. Methodological debates about the reliability of attributing the surge in inequality to trade or technology used theory and data, alternative methods of analysis, and the experiences of many countries. Yet in the end, the conclusion remained: that trade did not play a large role in altering inequality.

Using factor content analysis, Borjas, Freeman, and Katz (1997) found that trade explained an increase of 0.01 log points in the US college wage premium between 1980 and 1995, while the actual rise was 0.191 log points. Thus, they concluded that trade explained only a small fraction of the actual surge in inequality. Further, based on the theory, the higher wages of skilled workers relative to unskilled workers should have reduced the employment of high- relative to low-skilled workers in all the manufacturing sectors, while the incorporation into the labor force of the growing relative supply of college graduates should have occurred via reallocation of resources from less to more skill-intensive sectors. Yet, in the data, the employment of skilled workers relative to the unskilled increased in most manufacturing industries. This evidence appeared to be more consistent with ubiquitous skill-biased technical change than with trade, and more so in view of the fact that the rise of the skill premium was prevalent in countries at varying levels of development.

A variant of the factor proportions theory was also applied to the study of offshoring, with comparable results. Technological developments that made feasible the geographic separation of production tasks and the outsourcing of intermediate inputs affected the demand for different types of labor in multiple ways. Wright (2014) found that offshoring brought about a direct loss of low-skilled jobs in US manufacturing between 2001 and 2007 (defined as production workers), but that offshoring had a positive indirect effect on the employment of these workers due to an expansion of output prompted by the induced lower fabrication costs. As a result, the net job loss due to offshoring amounted to 69,000 workers, compared to the total loss of 1.2 million production jobs in the US manufacturing industries. Clearly, the job losses attributed by this study to offshoring were small compared to the total losses of employment. In addition, Feenstra and Hanson (1999), who studied the evolution of the wages of nonproduction relative to production workers in the US economy between 1979 and 1990, found that offshoring could explain an average of about 20 percent of the rise in this ratio. They reported three types of estimates, where the differences among them resulted from the use of different measures of high-technology capital. Explaining a fifth of the variation is of course significant, but it does not justify blaming globalization for all the ills of inequality.

As time went by, models of international trade with additional features were developed to study this issue. Matching theory was incorporated into trade models, enabling researchers to examine rich patterns in the response of compensation profiles to international conditions. In the new models, heterogeneous workers matched with heterogeneous managers, with various types of occupations, with different kinds of capital equipment, with firms that differed in technological characteristics, and with firms that served only the domestic market or engaged in foreign trade. Sophisticated models of this type were employed for quantitative analysis, addressing inequality in a single country or in a collection of countries that comprise the world economy.

Although these extensions introduced *rematching* as a new channel through which globalization could affect inequality, the quantitative impact of these innovations was found to be small. As a case in point, consider the Burstein, Morales, and Vogel (2016) study of the United

States, in which workers matched with two types of equipment and thirty occupations. In this data, workers were characterized by age, gender, and five educational categories. To measure inequality, the study considered the average wages of workers with a college degree relative to the average wages of workers without a college degree. Between 1984 and 2003, this skill premium increased by 28 percentage points. Burstein, Morales, and Vogel estimated that if there had been no disproportionately large increase in the demand for college graduates, the skill premium would have *declined*. But the demand shift in favor of educated workers brought about a rise in the inequality of earnings. Most of this demand shift was due to the expansion of computer usage, and a little less than one-fifth was due to an increased demand for occupations in which college graduates had a comparative advantage. The study also found that trade in equipment contributed 2.1 percentage points, and trade in occupation services contributed 1.3 percentage points, to the rise in the skill premium during that period. Evidently, these trade flows explain a small fraction, about 11 percent, of the data.

Rematching also played a major role in Lee's (2017) analysis, where five types of workers—distinguished by education level—sorted into four sectors and five occupations. Her structural model contained thirty-three countries at different levels of development. She found that the decline in the estimated trade costs between 2000 and 2007 brought about an increase in the average wages of workers in every education bracket. But the shift in the profile of real wages differed markedly across countries.

In some rich countries, inequality increased across all groups of workers (for example, Canada and Japan), and this also happened in some of the poorer countries (for example, China and Poland). In other countries, real wages increased most for workers with the lowest and the highest education levels (for example, Brazil and Israel). And in two countries—New Zealand and Switzerland—inequality declined across all groups. Lee's estimates showed that this lowering of trade costs can explain only 11.4 percent of the rise of the college wage premium in the United States from 2000 through 2007, and about 17 percent of the rise in China.

Several studies addressed the role of regional disparities in shaping inequality. These included research on the effects of NAFTA in the United States and of MERCOSUR in Brazil, the integration of China into the global economy, and the integration of republics from the former Soviet Union into the world's economy. The findings differed across countries. MERCOSUR brought about a *decline* in Brazil's regional wage inequality. China's integration into the world's trading system had a small effect on regional wage disparity in the United States but large effects on the disparity of regional employment levels and government transfers. China had almost no impact on regional disparity in Germany, while the eastern countries that gained independence from the Soviet Union had small effects on Germany's regional inequality.

To illustrate, Kovak (2013) estimated that MERCOSUR reduced the disparity in average wages between a Brazilian region in the 90th percentile of the wage distribution relative to a region in the 10th percentile of this distribution from 80 percent to 77 percent. And he found that this free trade agreement reduced the excess in average wages in the 75th percentile relative to the 25th percentile of the wage distribution from 36 percent to 35 percent. Namely, the trade agreement reduced regional wage disparity, but not by much. Kovak's work with Dix-Carneiro (2015) also examined the impact of MERCOSUR on regional skill premia, defined as the average wage of workers with a high school degree or more relative to workers with less than a high school education. The regional gaps in skill premia declined as a result of the free trade agreement, but not by much. Based on their estimates, the free trade agreement can explain about 14 percent of the decline in the skill premia between 1991 and 2000 in Brazil.

An influential study by Autor, Dorn, and Hanson (2013) examined the impact of the rise of China on the disparity of outcomes across US commuting zones (CZs). They found that China's surge had little impact on the variation in regional wages of manufacturing workers, but that workers in other sectors, mostly in services, suffered larger losses in more-affected regions. On the other hand, manufacturing *employment* declined more in the CZs that were more exposed to import competition from China, while no measurable employment differentials emerged in nonmanufacturing industries. Moreover, these authors did not find significant effects of the China shock on differences in regional population levels, but they did find considerable effects on differences in labor force participation and unemployment. The differences were larger for workers without a college degree than for workers with a college degree. Accounting for US *exports* to China reduced by a quarter the size of these estimates.

While Autor, Dorn, and Hanson compared average wages across the commuting zones, Chetverikov, Larsen, and Palmer (2016) examined inequality of wages within the CZs, dividing the wage distributions into twenty quantiles. In their analysis, there were no significant differences in wage responses above the medial quantile, and the largest negative effects surfaced in the second and third quantiles. These effects amounted to a 2.6 percent decline in earnings from 2000 to 2007 in the CZs that were exposed to the average size of the China shock.

These studies of regional divergences used difference-in-difference estimates under the assumption that workers did not relocate across commuting zones, even when they lost their jobs. In contrast, Caliendo, Dvorkin, and Parro (2015) used a structural model of the world economy, including the fifty US states, to study the impact of the China shock on regional disparities. Among the elements of their model, there were explicit moving costs for workers across the US states and sectors. They found that the China shock reduced manufacturing employment by 800,000 jobs over a ten-year period, but it increased employment in nonmanufacturing sectors by more. As a result, it *reduced* unemployment. The net employment gains were partly enabled by cheaper imports of intermediate inputs.

As I explained in Chapter 7, difference-in-difference estimates cannot be used per se to compute aggregate outcomes. For this reason, assumptions were made either about changes that occurred in a particular region or the average changes that occurred across regions, in order to construct the requisite aggregates. The resulting estimates were sensitive to these assumptions. Even the largest estimates of employment losses in US manufacturing due to the China surge were small relative to both the size of the US labor force and to the regular turnover of labor. From an aggregative point of view, the employment losses from this trade shock should have been easily accommodated in the regular course of business except that they were not; and import competition caused substantial pain in certain regions of the country.

Some of the new channels through which globalization affects inequality have not yet been properly quantified. One of them is the impact of scale. As Epifani and Gancia (2008) have shown, in a larger economy, due to domestic growth or to integration into the international system, labor demand can be biased in favor of skilled workers and thereby raise the skill premium and inequality. Although these authors found evidence for the impact of scale on inequality, their estimates cannot be used to quantify the fraction of the rise in inequality that was caused by this mechanism.

Grossman and Helpman (2018) described another mechanism, built on the heterogeneity of workers and firms, that could link inequality to globalization and growth. In their model, two features of the international economy play a central role. First, whether a country benefited directly—through the accumulation of usable knowledge—from research and development carried out by its trade partners. And second, whether international capital flows were free. In all cases, globalization raised the rate of growth of income per capita in all countries, with the possible exception of one, whose growth rate did

not change. In the presence of international R&D spillovers, globalization also raised inequality, independently of whether there was free
capital mobility. And in the absence of international R&D spillovers,
globalization had no impact on inequality in the absence of free borrowing and lending on international markets; and it *reduced* inequality in the presence of free borrowing and lending. Since no evidence
is available on these issues, these remain only theoretical possibilities
for the time being.

Another mechanism that links trade to inequality through firm
heterogeneity is selection into exporting, which bestows an advantage on more-productive firms in a globalized world. Since more-
productive firms use more skill-intensive technologies (as shown by
the evidence), then more openness to foreign trade, which induces
more firms to select into exporting, raises the relative demand for
skilled workers and thereby bids up the skill premium. The quantitative implications of this mechanism were studied by Burstein and
Vogel (2017) with a structural model that allowed factor intensities
to vary across industries as well as across firms within industries. In
one counterfactual exercise, they used the model to compare autarky
to the actual outcomes in 2005 through 2007. Similarly to Lee (2017),
they found that both skilled and unskilled workers gained from trade
in all the countries in their study (60 in total). Further, in all countries except Russia, trade increased wages of skilled workers relative
to wages of the unskilled, thereby increasing inequality. Nevertheless,
the estimated impacts were not large. Although the average rise of
the wage gap was 5.1 percent, it was 2 percent in the United States
and only 0.5 percent in Brazil. The largest increase was 12 percent, in
Lithuania.

Further extensions of the theory incorporated technology choice.
When combined with selection into exporting, the availability of
multiple technologies enabled firms that chose to export to also adopt
more-productive technologies, in line with the evidence. Under these
circumstances, globalization could generate income gains for low-

skilled workers and high-skilled workers proportionately more than for workers with intermediate skills, a pattern observed in some data sets. Globalization could also differentially change the composition of employment among firms of different productivity and size. In her study of MERCOSUR, Bustos (2011b) found that among Argentinian firms above the median size, a larger fraction exported than among firms below the median size. Bustos also found that in response to the free trade agreement, firms above the median increased by 6 percent their share of skilled workers, while firms below the median reduced their share of skilled workers by 8 percent. Her qualitative findings matched those predicted by the theory; however, she did not report the impact of these demand changes on wage inequality.

Biased technical change is yet another channel through which foreign trade can affect inequality. If globalization encourages the invention of technologies that raise the relative demand for skilled workers, it widens inequality. And if globalization encourages the invention of technologies that reduce the relative demand for skilled workers, it narrows inequality. Acemoglu (2003) calculated that technical change induced by globalization might have contributed about one-tenth of the rise in the US skill premium between 1980 and 1995, on top of another one-tenth rise due to the direct trade effect.

In a study of the impact of *offshoring* on induced technical change, Acemoglu, Gancia, and Zilibotti (2015) examined several scenarios. Of special interest is their calculation of the impact of a decline in the fixed costs of offshoring on the wages of skilled relative to unskilled US workers (that is, workers with some college education or more relative to workers with a high school education or less). In 2000, this wage ratio was 1.9. Namely, the skilled workers earned almost twice as much as the unskilled. The size of the decline in the fixed cost of offshoring was calibrated to generate an increase in the US volume of trade from its level in 2000 to the actual level in 2008. They found that this per se would have raised the wage ratio to 2.06. Evidently, according to this calculation, offshoring *together* with directed technical change contributed to the rise of the US skill premium between 2000 and 2008, but not by much.

All the studies mentioned so far in this chapter examined earnings inequality shaped by workers' observable characteristics. Of particular note was the emphasis on education levels, although differences in gender and experience were considered too. However, as argued in Chapter 10, much of the observed inequality and, even more so, of its increase over time were due to differences in the compensation of individuals with similar attributes. In Brazil, for example, observable worker characteristics explained only 13 percent of the variance in the log of wages in 1994 and only 2 percent of the increase in this variance between 1986 and 1995. Variation of wages across firms played a much bigger role, accounting for 39 percent of the variance in log wages in 1994 and for 86 percent of the increase in this variance between 1986 and 1995.

The question raised by this type of evidence is whether globalization might have increased wage dispersion within groups of workers with similar characteristics. To answer this question, economists developed various models that linked globalization to residual inequality. A central tenet of this theoretical work was that, in line with the evidence, larger and more-productive firms pay higher wages to similar employees. Under these circumstances, selection into exporting affects the distribution of wages, although not in a monotonic way. Helpman, Itskhoki, Muendler, and Redding (2017), who estimated a model of this type with Brazilian data, showed that trade liberalization raised residual inequality initially but that after reaching a peak, further trade liberalization reduced inequality. They found that reductions in variable trade costs could raise residual inequality by as much as 23.3 percent above autarky.

As is apparent from this short (and selective) review of the empirical findings, globalization in the form of foreign trade and offshoring has not been a large contributor to rising inequality. Multiple studies of different events around the world point to this conclusion. This is not to say, however, that reductions of barriers to trade have had no negative repercussions. They have, and these ill effects have been concentrated in certain regions of the United States. This concentration might be what provoked the political backlash against globalization.

Yet it is important to bear in mind that individual attitudes toward foreign trade and foreign business ties are positive overall. Using the PEW Global Attitudes survey, Pavcnik (2017) reported that more than half of the individuals in every one of the forty surveyed countries said in 2002 and in 2014 that foreign trade and foreign business ties were good for their country. Although this positive evaluation was lower in 2014 than in 2002, it remained high nevertheless. Further, in both years the support for globalization was negatively correlated with income per capita, suggesting that individuals in poorer countries viewed globalization more favorably than did individuals in richer countries.

Some important questions have not yet been satisfactorily answered, however, and reliable answers to these questions may change our view of the role of globalization in shaping inequality. First, what is the combined impact of all the channels of influence discussed in this book? We have seen that these influences are not additive, meaning that after estimating the impact of, say, two channels separately, we cannot just add up the estimates to obtain a combined effect. When globalization changes inequality via more than one channel, the combined effect can be highly nonlinear and these channels need to be jointly evaluated. At this point, there are no good tools for this type of analysis.

Second, as I discussed in the Introduction, international capital flows and migration also contribute to inequality. Although the latter has been studied extensively, we know little about the former. Further, both migration and capital mobility interact with foreign trade, offshoring, and foreign direct investment; and these interactions have the potential of producing combined effects on inequality that are different from the sum of their separate parts. No such studies of combined effects are available, however.

Another important area of inquiry concerns policy formation. Policies toward trade, migration, and capital flows are not divorced from each other. As a result, it is necessary to understand the political economy that shapes these policies in order to arrive at a broader appraisal of the impact on inequality of changes in any one of these areas. For example, the growing role of China in the global economy can induce policy changes in other countries. For this reason, estimates of the impact of the China shock on inequality will be biased if they do not account for such policy responses. Another example concerns differences in economic structure that have emerged between different countries, in Europe and in North America, as a result of varying political forces (see the discussion in Razin and Sadka 2014). Cross-country differences in political and socioeconomic institutions may help to explain differences in countries' responses to secular changes in trade and technology and thereby differences in inequality.

Political institutions and social norms influence deliberate redistribution policies. Governments engage in redistribution through taxes and transfers. This has two implications: First, inequality of market income is not the same as inequality of disposable income after accounting for taxes and transfers (see the discussion in Chapter 1). Second, a country's tax-transfer system may respond to changes in international conditions. As a consequence, global shocks affect inequality not only directly but also indirectly through induced changes in taxes and transfers. The focus of this book has been on inequality of market income, yet an analysis of the impact of globalization on the inequality of disposable income is of great interest. A recent study by Antràs, de Gortari, and Itskhoki (2017) illustrates this point.

Piketty (2014) argued that the two world wars played an important role in reducing inequality within countries, while Scheidel (2017) went further, arguing that throughout history violence was necessary for income and wealth equalization:

> For thousands of years, civilization did not lend itself to peaceful equalization. Across a wide range of societies and different levels of development, stability favored economic inequality. This was as true of Pharaonic Egypt as it was of Victorian England, as true of the Roman Empire as of the United States. Violent shocks were of paramount importance in disrupting the established order, in compressing the distribution of income and wealth, in narrowing the gap between rich and poor (p. 6).

This pessimistic view is quite extreme and hopefully exaggerates the role of violence in reducing inequality.

Most discussions of inequality concern comparisons of earnings. Nevertheless, what matters for the standard of living is real income. Inequality of earnings and inequality of real income are one and the same if the price indexes of consumption are the same for all individuals, independently of their income levels. This is the case when the composition of consumption does not vary with income. But if this is not the case, as shown by the evidence, then evaluating the impact of globalization on the price indexes of individuals in different income brackets in addition to the impact of globalization on their earnings is necessary to arrive at an estimate of the impact of globalization on the distribution of real income.

Although this is an underresearched area, Fajgelbaum, Grossman, and Helpman (2011) developed a theory of trade in products of varying quality in which the consumer price index differs for individuals with different income levels. Their model generates predictions about the quality patterns of importables and exportables across countries, in line with the evidence. In addition, a recent study by Fajgelbaum and Khandelwal (2016) showed that the variation in magnitude of the impact of trade on price indexes is large. In their study of forty countries, they found that going from autarky to trade reduced the consumer price index of individuals in the 10th percentile of the earnings distribution by 63 percent on average, and it reduced the consumer price index of individuals in the 90th percentile of the distribution of earnings by 28 percent on average, a ratio of 2.25. Although this ratio was larger than 1 in all countries, meaning that low-income individuals gained proportionately more through lower prices than did high-income individuals, this ratio was large in some countries and small in others. For example, it was more than 17 in the United States and 9 in Australia, but only 1.31 in Hungary and 1.07 in Luxemburg (see their table V). The main cause for these larger gains of low-income individuals was their consumption bias toward goods that were more traded on international markets. By these estimates, the impact of globalization on the cost of living *reduced* real income disparity.

Finally, we have seen that import competition from China did not have large aggregative effects in the United States, but it had substantially different employment repercussions in different commuting zones. The relative reductions of employment were regionally concentrated, as were transfers from programs such as the Trade Adjustment Assistance (TAA) program, Unemployment Benefits and Disability Insurance. The pain caused to particular individuals by job losses—which is hidden from the eyes of the statistician—can be substantial. Goldstein's (2017) account of the impact of the closure of a General Motors plant in Janesville, Wisconsin, portrays the painful and distressing fallout of this decision on some of the local residents. It also makes clear the need for safety nets that shield individuals from trade and other types of shocks to local economies. The US TAA program was designed to help workers who lose their jobs due to import competition. But this program is small and inadequate for handling large localized import shocks. Moreover, as shown by Kletzer (2001), workers who lost employment between 1979 and 1994 as a result of import competition were not very different from workers who lost jobs for other reasons, such as automation or shifts in demand. For this reason, it is necessary to build safety nets for workers who lose jobs, independently of whether the job losses are caused by foreign competition. This is a major challenge for public policy.

In summary, there remain important outstanding issues in the study of globalization and inequality. Yet it is important to bear in mind that great progress has been made on this front. Changes in the international economy and in the organization of production around the world have introduced new challenges that have been faced head-on by scholars from multiple fields of economics, who have provided improved and more refined answers to many pertinent questions in this area. Although the public debate about the costs and benefits of globalization is not over, one can only hope that it will be based on evidence and that the evidence reported in this book will play a useful role.

Notes

Chapter 1. Historical Background

1. I thank Alan Taylor for providing the updated data on which Figure 1.1 is based.

2. Figure 1.2 uses data from the World Bank, which differ in various ways from the Maddison (1995, 2001) data that was used for Figure 1.1. The World Bank data are more comprehensive and show larger values of trade-to-income ratios.

3. Bourguignon and Morrisson (2002) provided the first analysis of inequality around the globe, and their calculations have been updated by Morrisson and Murtin (2011). My analysis uses data from van Zanden, Baten, Foldvari, and van Leeuwen (2014), which also builds on the original Bourguignon and Morrisson study but enriches it substantially. See Milanovic (2016) for more details.

4. These data consist of the population-weighted natural logarithm of the ratio of a group's income share to its population share. The Theil index is only one index of inequality used in the literature. Another index is the Gini coefficient. These two indexes happen to be highly correlated. Other measures of inequality are percentile ratios, such as the 90th relative to the 10th percentile of the income distribution.

5. The U-shaped evolution of income inequality in the United States during the twentieth century also applies to other measures of income and

other measures of inequality, such as the top decile or top 1 percent income share (see Atkinson, Piketty, and Saez 2011), or the inverse Pareto-
Lorenz coefficient (reported in The World Wealth and Income Database,
http://www.wid.world, accessed on December 7, 2015).

6. Morrisson and Murtin (2011) report measures of extreme poverty
from 1700 to 2008. According to their estimates (see their table 3), extreme
poverty rates modestly declined during the eighteenth and nineteenth centuries.

7. The significance of capital has increased both because the share of
capital in national income has increased and because capital ownership has
become more concentrated. Note, however, that capital ownership includes
pension funds that belong to workers.

Chapter 2. The Rise of the College Wage Premium

1. This U-shaped pattern also obtains for other measures of inequality,
such as the Gini coefficient.

2. Katz and Autor (1999) report in their table 10 the log of these relative
wages, while Table 2.1 here reports the relative wages themselves that were
computed from their data.

3. I thank David Autor for providing the data for Figure 2.1.

4. See Bourguignon (2015, chap. 3) for a review of evidence concerning
these factors in a variety of countries.

5. Globalization can affect labor force participation in addition to wages
(see Chapter 7 for the evidence). For this reason, changes in relative wages
may underestimate the impact of trade exposure on inequality.

6. This argument is exact if there are only two sectors that produce with
constant returns to scale, the two countries have identical technologies, no
other inputs are required for production, and preferences are the same and
homothetic.

7. A number of less-developed countries, such as Brazil and India, had
trade reforms in the early 1990s that entailed tariff reductions on manufactured products. Other countries, such as China, joined the WTO later (China
joined in 2001).

8. In Stolper and Samuelson (1941), the economies were assumed to include two constant-returns-to-scale sectors and two factors of production,

labeled labor and capital. Moreover, one sector was capital intensive and the other was labor intensive, in the sense that the former used more capital per worker for a given wage rate and rental rate on capital. Under these circumstances, an increase in the price of labor-intensive products raises the real wage and reduces the real reward to capital. An increase in the price of capital-intensive products has the opposite effects. The same logic applies, of course, when instead of labor and capital, the economy uses skilled and unskilled workers. An extension of this result is provided in Jones and Scheinkman (1977); they showed that with many types of inputs and many types of sectors, all producing under constant returns to scale, an increase in the price of a product raises the real reward of some inputs and reduces the real reward of some other inputs.

9. Indeed, an analysis of the impact of trade protection on wages was the original motivation for Stolper and Samuelson (1941), who assumed that one sector is labor intensive and the other is capital intensive. A tariff raises the domestic price of import-competing products, as a result of which labor gains when the import-competing sector is labor intensive and labor loses when the import-competing sector is capital intensive. See Jones (1965) for an elegant demonstration.

Interestingly, while the Stolper-Samuelson theorem states that the relatively abundant type of labor gains from foreign trade while the relatively scarce type of labor loses, the gains from trade theorem states that in a Heckscher-Ohlin type economy (and more generally, too) there are *aggregate* gains from trade (see Helpman 2011, chap. 3). This means that by expanding the choice of consumption possibilities, trade enables the gainers to compensate the losers in a way that results in higher real income for every worker.

10. Rodrik (2015) provides an excellent discussion of this use of models in other areas of economics.

Chapter 3. Early Studies

1. Factor content analysis was first introduced by Leontief (1953), and its theoretical foundations were developed by Vanek (1968).

2. The term *notional* country is borrowed from Krugman (2008).

3. This analysis uses the following assumptions: The same technologies are used to produce domestic exportable products at home and abroad, the

same technologies are used to produce domestic import–competing products at home and abroad, and factor prices—such as the wages of skilled or unskilled workers—are the same at home and abroad. For an analysis that relaxes some of these assumptions, see Trefler (1995) and Davis and Weinstein (2001).

4. Katz and Murphy (1992) employed only the direct use of inputs in the calculation of the factor content of trade, which omits indirect impacts through intermediate inputs. Omitting intermediate inputs alters factor content estimates in important ways, however; see Davis and Weinstein (2001) and Trefler and Zhu (2010).

5. This is a bit higher than the rise in the college wage premium in Autor's (2014) data. In Autor's data the college wage premium was 49.4% in 1980 and it increased to 80.3% in 1995. The difference between the log of 1.803 and the log of 1.494 is 0.188, which is a bit smaller than 0.191. Some of this difference results from a difference in the definitions. Borjas, Freeman, and Katz include half of the workers with some college education in the group of high school graduates and the remaining half in the group of college graduates.

6. Note that the 3.1 elasticity of substitution between high school graduates and high school dropouts is larger than the 1.41 elasticity of substitution between college graduates and high school graduates. This means that high school graduates are better substitutes in production for high school dropouts than for college graduates.

7. The Stolper-Samuelson mechanism was also employed by Krugman (1995) for evaluating the influence of trade with less-developed countries on wages. Krugman argued that although in theory this mechanism can explain the empirical pattern, reasonable parametrization of the theoretical model led him to conclude that it cannot explain the *magnitude* of the rise in the college wage premium.

8. To obtain this result, Houthakker assumed that the relative productivity of capital varies across firms according to a Pareto distribution.

9. Oberfield and Raval (2014) study the relationship between the aggregate elasticity of substitution and its microeconomic determinants in a model with monopolistic competition. They show that in an economy with equal constant demand elasticities in all sectors and equal and constant elasticities of substitution between labor and capital in all sectors, the aggregate elas-

ticity of substitution between labor and capital is a weighted average of the demand elasticity and the elasticity of substitution.

Chapter 4. Trade versus Technology

1. There was a controversy surrounding these estimates. For example, Sachs and Shatz (1994) found a positive effect by isolating the computer industry. They justified this formulation with the argument that computer prices were mismeasured.

2. This formula provides a first-order approximation of the relationship between product price changes, changes in factor prices, and changes in technology. When these changes are not small, a second-order approximation can be used, which brings in additional variables.

3. Berman, Bound, and Machin (1998) provided a related analysis.

4. There are some finer points to consider in this analysis, for which the reader is referred to Krugman (2000). Moreover, in a more general setup, both factor-biased or factor-saving and sector-biased technical change may be relevant. See Xu (2001) for a clear analysis.

5. I have excluded Luxembourg and Japan, which had shares in excess of 100 percent.

Chapter 5. Offshoring

1. Baldwin described three phases of globalization: The first, referred to as the "first unbundling," started in the nineteenth century and was driven by declining costs of shipping; the second phase, referred to as the "second unbundling," started in the 1980s and was driven by declining costs of fragmentation; and the third phase, referred to as the "third unbundling," will take place mostly in the future and will be driven by declining costs of face-to-face interaction of individuals in different geographical locations.

2. The series ends just before the collapse of world trade as a result of the financial crisis that started in 2008.

3. Grossman and Rossi-Hansberg (2008) also show that the productivity effect is small when the range of offshored tasks is small. Yet the productivity effect can outweigh the price and labor-supply effects when the volume of offshoring is large.

4. Wright (2014) used the narrow index of offshoring that had been developed by Feenstra and Hanson (1999). See the discussion of Feenstra and Hanson's work below.

5. See, however, the discussion in Chapter 6 of Autor, Dorn, and Hanson (2013), who estimated the impact of all Chinese imports on US employment (including final goods and intermediate inputs), not only of imports that stemmed from offshoring.

6. Wright (2014) did not provide direct estimates of the impact of offshoring on productivity. But his employment estimates suggest that they were most likely significant.

7. Multiplying the annual change by 100 is done for convenience, to make numbers easier to read.

8. I am indebted to Robert Johnson for providing the data for this graph prior to the publication of his paper with Guillermo Noguera.

9. A key improvement in the Feenstra-Hanson estimation procedure was the isolation of the separate contributions of offshoring and technology (in the form of computers and other forms of high-tech capital equipment) to price changes, and using these price changes for estimating the mandated wage responses.

Chapter 6. Matching Workers with Jobs

1. To see that in the absence of complementarity "mixed" marriages—between spouses with characteristics 1 and 2—can yield the highest surplus, consider the case in which the surplus equals the value of the largest characteristic in the marriage. Then under PAM, the low-characteristics pair produces a surplus of 1 while the high-characteristics pair produces a surplus of 2, which adds up to a total surplus of 3. In a mixed marriage, the surplus equals 2 and there can be two such marriages. Therefore, in this case the aggregate surplus equals 4, which is larger than the aggregate surplus under PAM. In this example, complementarity does not hold, because raising by one unit the characteristic of the lower-index spouse does not raise the surplus.

2. For this condition to be necessary and sufficient for the inequality results derived in these studies, characteristics and quantities of the two parties have to interact in specific ways; see Eeckhout and Kircher (2018).

3. The rise of inequality in these circumstances is very pronounced, because the wage inequality between every pair of workers with different ability levels rises. As a result, every index of inequality that respects mean-adjusted second-order stochastic dominance, such as the Theil index, rises as well.

4. An earlier variant by Ohnsorge and Trefler (2007) studied trade and wages with an assignment model in which workers, who differed in two attributes, are sorted across sectors.

5. Generally speaking, with many ability levels, it is possible for one country to have relatively more higher-ability workers at the lower end of the ability distribution but relatively fewer higher-ability workers at the upper end of the ability distribution, as well as more complicated patterns of relative abundance of abilities.

6. Grossman and Maggi (2000) provided the first theoretical analysis of the impact of diversity on trade flows. Bombardini, Gallipoli, and Pupato (2012) provided empirical evidence. See Grossman (2013) for a review of this literature.

7. A firm's production function is separable in quantities and abilities of inputs in a way that makes total factor productivity dependent only on abilities, and it exhibits constant returns to scale in quantities.

8. I am grateful to Anders Akerman for providing the data for Figure 6.2.

9. The original sector-specific model was developed by Jones (1971). In his version, there are two sectors and three inputs. One input is trapped in one sector, another is trapped in the other sector. They are called sector-specific inputs, because they cannot reallocate across industries. The third factor is footloose and can costlessly move from one industry to the other. In this framework, an increase in the price of a product raises the reward to the sector-specific input manufacturing this product and reduces the reward to the other sector-specific input.

10. In the sector-specific model, the sector-specific inputs cannot change their sector of employment, as explained in the previous footnote, while here they can. Nevertheless, the ability level of an input affects its sectoral comparative advantage; hence, the semispecificity.

11. The joint distribution of worker wages and the earnings of managers is not examined in this study.

12. Naturally, wherever matching improves for labor, it deteriorates for managers, and vice versa.

13. An interesting model of matching between workers and managers, which has so far not been sufficiently explored for the study of globalization, was developed by Kremer and Maskin (1996). They studied a simple technological structure in which output is produced by a team of two individuals, each one assigned to a different task. The two tasks can be viewed as management and fabrication, or production and nonproduction. Each task can be performed by individuals with different ability (skill) levels; but the tasks are complementary, and the elasticity of output with respect to ability differs across the tasks. The labor force consists of individuals with varying discrete ability levels. The model showed that in an economy of this type with a competitive labor market, an increase in the mean ability of the workforce reduces wage inequality when the ability distribution is not too dispersed, and it raises wage inequality when the distribution of ability is highly dispersed (here the term wages is used for the compensation of managers and workers). These results are related to the model's finding that rising dispersion of abilities within the population reduces the dispersion of skills within firms, that is, the ability of the manager relative to the ability of the worker declines. Maskin (2015) used this model to illustrate by example how globalization can raise wage inequality in a poor country that is populated by individuals with lower ability levels than its trade partner. Similarly to Antràs, Garicano, and Rossi-Hansberg (2006), he assumed that globalization allows individuals from different countries to be matched with each other.

14. The latter is formalized as a Fréchet distribution, which has become common in studies of international trade since its introduction into the trade literature by Eaton and Kortum (2002). To ensure sharp results, the authors build in complementarity relationships between workers, equipment, and occupations, using a stochastic version of log supermodularity. A similar specification of comparative advantage of workers across sectors, which leads to sectoral sorting of workers, was first introduced by Lagakos and Waugh (2013) in their analysis of structural transformation.

15. The education levels are: high school dropouts, high school graduates, some college completed, college completed, and graduate training. The age groups are: 17 to 30, 31 to 43, and 44 and older.

16. This is a bit lower than the college wage premium in Autor's (2014) data, where the college wage premium is defined as wages of workers with a college degree relative to workers with a high school degree. In Autor's data, the college wage premium was 58 percent in 1984 and 86 percent in 2003, which yields log(1.86) – log(1.58) = 0.164. I thank Jonathan Vogel for clarifying this point.

17. As in Burstein, Morales, and Vogel (2016), these productivities are drawn from a Fréchet distribution. Unlike their model, however, Lee allows the shape and location parameters to depend on a worker's type.

18. Lee (2017) defined the college wage premium as the ratio of these two average wages, which is different from the definition used by Burstein, Morales, and Vogel (2016). To understand the difference, consider a case in which the ratio of these average wages is 1.5. Then 1.5 is the college wage premium according to Lee and 50 percent according to Burstein, Morales, and Vogel. This difference in definitions has implications for the evaluation of the size of changes in the college wage premium. An increase in the relative wages from 1.5 to 1.545 amounts to a 3 percent rise according to Lee's definition but to a 9 percent increase according to the Burstein, Morales, and Vogel definition. In general, the former definition yields smaller numbers for the rise in the skill premium than does the latter.

19. The following discussion is based on a table provided by Eunhee Lee in private communication, which is comparable in structure to table A3 in her paper. I am grateful to her for providing these data and for clarifying various queries concerning her estimates.

Chapter 7. Regional Disparity

1. Due to lack of data, Kovak (2013) assumed that the elasticity of substitution between labor and the sector-specific input equaled 1 in each one of his 21 sectors. Moreover, he extended the analysis to include nontraded goods, which were included in the sectoral structure.

2. I am indebted to Brian Kovak for providing these estimates in private communication. It is important to note that these numbers are based on residual regional wage estimates, after controlling for workers' observable characteristics. Nevertheless, similar estimates were obtained using raw wage data.

3. Brazil had a large informal sector in which mostly small firms operated, paying lower wages.

4. For example, Trefler (2004) found that in response to the 1989 Canada–US free trade agreement most of the employment adjustments worked out within a three-year period.

5. See Romalis (2007), who found a zero net effect on the United States, and Caliendo and Parro (2015) who found very small positive effects for each one of the NAFTA partners: Canada, Mexico, and the United States.

6. The Balassa RCA index for sector i is defined as the share of sector i in a country's exports divided by the share of sector i in the world's exports. Under this definition, a disproportionately large share of a country's exports in sector i (RCA larger than 1) displays a comparative advantage in this sector; and a disproportionately small share (RCA smaller than 1) displays a comparative disadvantage.

7. These data are from WTO (2016, table A4). In the same publication, table A5 provides estimates of import shares. China's share of merchandise imports increased from 6.9 percent in 1973 to 10.3 percent in 2015.

8. According to Autor, Dorn, and Hanson (2013, p. 2139), "Chinese import exposure rose by $1,140 per worker between 1990 and 2000 and by an additional $1,839 per worker in the seven years between 2000 and 2007."

9. Ebenstein, Harrison, McMillan, and Phillips (2014), who studied sectoral outcomes, also found no significant effects of import competition on the wages of US workers in manufacturing industries.

10. Between 1988 and 2008, import exposure per worker increased by 6,147 euros, while export exposure per worker increased by 7,060 euros.

11. In the usual economic terminology, upstream refers to sectors providing an industry with inputs, while downstream refers to sectors purchasing inputs from the industry. Input–output tables are used for identifying these linkages.

12. Pierce and Schott (2016) also engaged in a sectoral analysis in order to assess the impact of China's export surge after its accession to the WTO in 2001. Unlike Acemoglu, Autor, Dorn, Hanson, and Price (2016), however, they used the gap between the tariffs that Chinese imports would have faced if they had not been afforded the Normal Trade Relations (NTR) status (which entitles a country to tariff levels under the WTO's Most Favored Na-

tion clause) and the NTR status that they were actually afforded. Since this status was renewed annually, the risk of nonrenewal curtailed Chinese exports to the United States (China was granted permanent NTR status with its accession to the WTO). Because this gap varied across industries, Pierce and Schott could use difference-in-difference methods to estimate the impact of the gap on changes in employment differences across industries. They found substantial cross-sectoral variation: The disparity in employment declines amounted to 0.08 log points between an industry in the 75th percentile of the distribution of the NTR gaps and the 25th percentile of the distribution, which is about 8.3 percent.

13. "[W]e define the exposed sector to encompass all manufacturing industries for which predicted import exposure rose by at least 2 percentage points between 1991 and 2011, as well as all industries (both within and outside of manufacturing) for which the predicted full upstream import exposure measure increased by at least 4 percentage points over 1991–2011. . . . we next subdivide the nonexposed sector into tradables and nontradables. In our nomenclature, tradable industries are those that produce tradable goods or commodities and specifically constitute the manufacturing, agriculture, forestry, fishing, and mining sectors. We classify all other sectors, including services, as nontradable, though this approach is admittedly imperfect since some services are also traded" (pp. S177–S178). Predicted import exposure is computed from the first-stage equation in their two-stage estimation procedure.

14. I am grateful to Daron Acemoglu for clarifying this point in private communication.

15. Source: Federal Reserve Economic Data (FRED) https://fred .stlouisfed.org/search?st=employment, accessed on May 28, 2017.

16. Davis and von Wachter (2011) also reported large employer-initiated separations in the US economy. According to data from the Job Openings and Labor Turnover Survey (JOLTS), between 1990 and 2011 there were on average 9 million layoffs per quarter among nonfarm payroll employees.

17. Calibrated parameters are chosen to ensure that the model fits certain features of the data, often referred to as "moments" of the data.

18. An explicit theoretical model can in certain cases deliver an estimation equation that avoids some of the pitfalls of the above-discussed approaches.

The work of Acemoglu and Restrepo (2017), who studied the effects of the introduction of industrial robots into the US economy on employment and wages in commuting zones (CZs), illustrates this point. They derived an equation that related the sectoral penetration of robots to CZ employment levels and used it to estimate a *derived* parameter (a parameter that is a function of other parameters of the model) that was needed for computing the aggregate loss of jobs. Yet this parameter was not sufficient for this purpose. They therefore introduced into the analysis additional parameters, obtained from *other* sources, which together with their estimated parameter could be used to calculate the aggregate effect. Although this approach uses an explicit theoretical model, which is essential, it does not require full knowledge of its details.

19. Artuc, Chaudhuri, and McLaren (2010) studied switching costs of this type for sectoral mobility in the United States and found that they were substantial.

Chapter 8. Firm Characteristics

1. See Krugman (1979), Lancaster (1979, chap. 10), Dixit and Norman (1980 chap. 9), Helpman (1981), and Ethier (1982) for the original contributions to this trade theory.

2. These assumptions preclude fixed expenditure shares in consumption or constant cost shares in the variable costs of production, which are often used for convenience but require elasticities of substitution equal to 1.

3. Mincerian estimates of the returns to schooling are obtained by regressing the log of wages on years of schooling, controlling for other worker characteristics such as experience and gender.

4. The data coverage was not the same in the two cases. Mincerian returns to education were available for forty countries, with years of observation differing across the countries from 1962 through 1995. Manufacturing skill premia were available for thirty-five countries in 1980 and 1990. I am grateful to Gino Gancia for clarifying these points in private correspondence.

5. An alternative, less-influential model was developed by Bernard, Eaton, Jensen, and Kortum (2003). See, however, Burstein and Vogel (2017) for an interesting application.

6. See Melitz and Redding (2014) for a review of this model and its many extensions.

7. Once the fixed export cost is low enough to induce all incumbent firms to export, the variable trade costs have no effect on inequality, and inequality is higher the larger the fixed cost of exporting.

8. Firms that engage in Bertrand competition react to the prices of their rivals. When multiple suppliers offer the same product and marginal costs of production do not vary with output, the game-theoretic outcome is that the lowest-cost firm charges a price equal to the next-lowest marginal cost and supplies the entire market.

9. See Helpman (2004 chap. 5) for a review of estimates of international R&D spillovers, which are quite large.

Chapter 9. Technology Choice

1. Krusell, Ohanian, Ríos-Rull, and Violante (2000) showed that capital accumulation can also bias wages in favor of skilled relative to unskilled workers, if highly skilled workers and machines and equipment are complementary in production. Their quantitative analysis suggests that this effect was large.

2. Bustos (2011a) studied the impact of MERCOSUR on the technology upgrading of Argentinian firms. She found that most of the upgrading occurred within firms that switched from nonexporting to exporting status in response to the free trade agreement.

3. He credited several previous studies with the suggestion that foreign trade modified labor productivity (see Wood 1994, p. 108).

4. See Grossman and Helpman (1991a) and Aghion and Howitt (1992) for the original models of economic growth with quality ladders, and Grossman and Helpman (1991a,b) for their application to issues of trade and growth. Acemoglu (1998) had developed some of the insights that were used in Acemoglu (2003).

5. Acemoglu (2003) assumed parameter restrictions that made innovation unprofitable in the less-developed countries.

6. See Grossman and Helpman (1991a,b) for a comparison of the quality ladder versus the expanding product variety growth mechanisms and their

application to international trade. Helpman (2004, chap. 4) provides a non-technical review. The original expanding product variety growth model was developed by Romer (1990).

7. This type of tradeoff is known as the *proximity–concentration tradeoff* in the literature on foreign direct investment; see Helpman (2011, chap. 6).

8. These results were derived under the assumption that the elasticity of substitution between intermediates was larger than the elasticity of substitution between low-skill–intensive and high-skill–intensive products, and that the latter elasticity of substitution was larger than 1. These assumptions, which the authors considered to be plausible, were similar to the assumptions used in Acemoglu (2003).

Chapter 10. Residual Inequality

1. Helpman, Itskhoki, and Redding (2010) used a bargaining game between the firm and its workers to describe wage setting. In the solution to this game, a firm's wage rate is a fraction of its revenue per worker, and this fraction is a function of two parameters: one representing the curvature of the revenue function, the other representing the curvature of the production function.

References

Acemoglu, Daron. 1998. "Why Do New Technologies Complement Skills? Directed Technical Change and Wage Inequality." *Quarterly Journal of Economics* 113: 1055–1089.

———. 2003. "Patterns of Skill Premia." *Review of Economic Studies* 70: 199–230.

Acemoglu, Daron, David Autor, David Dorn, Gordon H. Hanson, and Brendan Price. 2016. "Import Competition and the Great US Employment Sag of the 2000s." *Journal of Labor Economics* 34: S141–S198.

Acemoglu, Daron, Gino Gancia, and Fabrizio Zilibotti. 2015. "Offshoring and Directed Technical Change." *American Economic Journal: Macroeconomics* 7: 84–122.

Acemoglu, Daron, and Pascual Restrepo. 2017. "Robots and Jobs: Evidence from US Labor Markets." National Bureau of Economic Research Working Paper 23285.

Aghion, Philippe, and Peter Howitt. 1992. "A Model of Growth Through Creative Destruction." *Econometrica* LX: 323–351.

Akerman, Anders, Elhanan Helpman, Oleg Itskhoki, Marc-Andreas Muendler, and Stephen Redding. 2013. "Sources of Wage Inequality." *American Economic Review* (Papers and Proceedings) 103: 214–219.

Amiti, Mary, and Donald R. Davis. 2012. "Trade, Firms, and Wages: Theory and Evidence." *Review of Economic Studies* 79: 1–36.

Anand, Sudhir, and Paul Segal. 2015. "The Global Distribution of Income." Chapter 11 in Anthony B. Atkinson and Francois Bourguignon (eds.), *Handbook of Income Distribution*, Vol. 2A (Amsterdam: North–Holland).

Antràs, Pol. 2016. *Global Production: Firms, Contracts, and Trade Structure* (Princeton: Princeton University Press).

Antràs, Pol, Alonso de Gortari, and Oleg Itskhoki. 2017. "Globalization, Inequality and Welfare." *Journal of International Economics* 108: 387–412.

Antràs, Pol, Luis Garicano, and Esteban Rossi-Hansberg. 2006. "Offshoring in a Knowledge Economy." *Quarterly Journal of Economics* 121: 31–77.

Artuc, Erhan, Shubham Chaudhuri, and John McLaren. 2010. "Trade Shocks and Labor Adjustment: A Structural Empirical Approach." *American Economic Review* 100: 1008–1045.

Atkinson, Anthony B., Thomas Piketty, and Emmanuel Saez. 2011. "Top Incomes in the Long Run of History." *Journal of Economic Literature* 49: 3–71.

Autor, David H. 2014. "Skills, Education, and the Rise of Earnings Inequality Among the 'Other 99 percent.'" *Science* 344: 843–851.

Autor, David H., David Dorn, and Gordon H. Hanson. 2013. "The China Syndrome: Local Labor Market Effects of Import Competition in the United States." *American Economic Review* 103: 2121–2168.

Autor, David H., David Dorn, Gordon H. Hanson, and Jae Song. 2014. "Trade Adjustment: Worker Level Evidence." *Quarterly Journal of Economics* 129: 1799–1860.

Autor, David H., Lawrence F. Katz, and Melissa Schettini Kearney. 2008. "Trends in U.S. Wage Inequality: Revising the Revisionists." *Review of Economics and Statistics* 90: 300–323.

Autor, David H., Lawrence F. Katz, and Alan Krueger. 1998. "Computing Inequality: Have Computers Changed the Labor Market?" *Quarterly Journal of Economics* 113: 1169–1214.

Autor, David H., Alan Manning, and Christopher L. Smith. 2016. "The Contribution of the Minimum Wage to US Wage Inequality over Three Decades: A Reassessment." *American Economic Journal: Applied Economics* 8: 58–99.

Balassa, Bela. 1965. "Trade Liberalization and 'Revealed' Comparative Advantage." *Manchester School* 33: 99–123.

Baldwin, Richard. 2016. *The Great Convergence: Information Technology and the New Globalization* (Cambridge, MA: The Belknap Press of Harvard University Press).

Becker, Gary. 1973. "A Theory of Marriage I." *Journal of Political Economy* 81: 813–846.

Berman, Eli, John Bound, and Zvi Griliches. 1994. "Changes in the Demand for Skilled Labor in U.S. Manufacturing Industries: Evidence from the Annual Survey of Manufacturing." *Quarterly Journal of Economics* 109: 367–398.

Berman, Eli, John Bound, and Stephen Machin. 1998. "Implications of Skill-Biased Technological Change: International Implications." *Quarterly Journal of Economics* 113: 1245–1279.

Berman, Eli, and Stephen Machin. 2000. "Skill-Biased Technology Transfer Around the World." *Oxford Review of Economic Policy* 16: 12–22.

Bernard, Andrew B., Jonathan Eaton, J. Bradford Jensen, and Samuel Kortum. 2003. "Plants and Productivity in International Trade." *American Economic Review* 93: 1268–1290.

Bernard, Andrew B., and J. Bradford Jensen. 1995. "Exporters, Jobs, and Wages in U.S. Manufacturing, 1976–1987." *Brookings Papers on Economic Activity: Microeconomics*: 67–112.

———. 1999. "Exceptional Exporter Performance: Cause, Effect, or Both?" *Journal of International Economics* 47: 1–25.

Bernard, Andrew B., J. Bradford Jensen, Stephen J. Redding, and Peter K. Schott. 2016. "Global Firms." National Bureau of Economic Research Working Paper 22727, forthcoming in the *Journal of Economic Literature*.

Bhagwati, Jagdish. 1988. *Protectionism* (Cambridge, MA: The MIT Press).

———. 2002. *Free Trade Today* (Princeton: Princeton University Press).

Blau, Francine D., and Lawrence M. Kahn. 2015. "Immigration and the Distribution of Incomes." In Barry R. Chiswick and Paul W. Miller (eds.), *Handbook of the Economics of International Migration* Vol. 1A (Amsterdam: North Holland).

Bombardini, Matilde, Giovanni Gallipoli, and Germán Pupato. 2012. "Skill Dispersion and Trade Flows." *American Economic Review* 102: 2327–2348.

Borjas, George J., Richard B. Freeman, and Lawrence F. Katz. 1997. "How Much Do Immigration and Trade Affect Labor Market Outcome?" *Brookings Papers on Economic Activity* 1: 1–90.

Bourguignon, François. 2015. *The Globalization of Inequality* (Princeton: Princeton University Press).

Bourguignon, François, and Christian Morrisson. 2002. "Inequality Among World Citizens: 1820–1992." *American Economic Review* 92: 727–744.

Burstein, Ariel, and Jonathan Vogel. 2017. "International Trade, Technology, and the Skill Premium." *Journal of Political Economy* 125: 1356–1412.

Burstein, Ariel, Eduardo Morales, and Jonathan Vogel. 2016. "Changes in Between-Group Inequality: Computers, Occupations, and International Trade." Mimeo, September 13.

Bustos, Paula. 2011a. "Trade Liberalization, Exports, and Technology Upgrading: Evidence on the Impact of MERCOSUR on Argentinean Firms." *American Economic Review* 101: 304–340.

———. 2011b. "The Impact of Trade Liberalization on Skill Upgrading: Evidence from Argentina." Barcelona Graduate School of Economics Working Paper: 559.

Caliendo, Lorenzo, and Fernando Parro. 2015. "Estimates of the Trade and Welfare Effects of NAFTA." *Review of Economic Studies* 82: 1–44.

Caliendo, Lorenzo, Maximiliano Dvorkin, and Fernando Parro. 2015. "Trade and Labor Market Dynamics." Mimeo, November 2015.

Card, David. 2009. "Immigration and Inequality." *American Economic Review* (Papers and Proceedings) 99 (2): 1–21.

Card, David, and John E. DiNardo. 2002. "Skill-Biased Technological Change and Rising Wage Inequality: Some Problems and Puzzles." *Journal of Labor Economics* 20: 733–783.

Chamberlin, Edward H. 1933. *The Theory of Monopolistic Competition* (Cambridge, MA: Harvard University Press).

Chandy, Laurence, and Brian Seidel. 2016. "Is Globalization's Second Wave About to Break?" Global Views No. 4, The Brookings Institution.

Chetverikov, Denis, Bradley Larsen, and Christopher Palmer. 2016. "IV Quantile Regression for Group-Level Treatments, with an Application to the Distributional Effects of Trade." *Econometrica* 84: 809–833.

Costinot, Arnaud, and Jonathan Vogel. 2010. "Matching and Inequality in the World Economy." *Journal of Political Economy* 118: 747–785.

Council of Economic Advisors. 2016. *Economic Report of the President* (Washington, DC).

Dauth, Wolfgang, Sebastian Findeisen, and Jens Suedekum. 2014. "The Rise of the East and the Far East: German Labor Markets and Trade Integration." *Journal of the European Economic Association* 12: 1643–1675.

Davidson, Carl, Steven J. Matusz, and Andrei Shevchenko. 2008. "Globalization and Firm Level Adjustment with Imperfect Labor Markets." *Journal of International Economics* 75: 295–309.

Davis, Donald R., and David W. Weinstein. 2001. "An Account of Global Factor Trade." *American Economic Review* 91: 1423–1453.

Davis, Donald R., and James Harrigan. 2011. "Good Jobs, Bad Jobs, and Trade Liberalization." *Journal of International Economics* 84: 26–36.

Davis, Steven J., and Till von Wachter. 2011. "Recessions and the Costs of Job Loss." *Brookings Papers on Economic Activity*, Fall: 1–72.

Diamond, Peter A. 1982a. "Demand Management in Search Equilibrium." *Journal of Political Economy* 90: 881–894.

———. 1982b. "Wage Determination and Efficiency in Search Equilibrium." *Review of Economic Studies* 49: 217–227.

Dix-Carneiro, Rafael, and Brian K. Kovak. 2015. "Trade Liberalization and the Skill Premium: A Local Labor Market Approach." *American Economic Review (Papers and Proceedings)* 105: 551–557.

———. 2017. "Trade Liberalization and Regional Dynamics." *American Economic Review* 107: 2908–2946.

Dixit, Avinash, and Victor Norman. 1980. *The Theory of International Trade* (Cambridge, UK: Cambridge University Press).

Dixit, Avinash, and Joseph E. Stiglitz. 1977. "Monopolistic Competition and Optimum Product Diversity." *American Economic Review* 67: 297–308.

Eaton, Jonathan, and Samuel Kortum. 2002. "Technology, Geography, and Trade." *Econometrica* 70: 1741–1779.

Ebenstein, Avraham, Ann Harrison, Margaret McMillan, and Shannon Phillips. 2014. "Estimating the Impact of Trade and Offshoring on American Workers Using the Current Population Surveys." *Review of Economics and Statistics* 96: 581–595.

Eeckhout, Jan, and Philipp Kircher. 2018. "Assortative Matching with Large Firms." *Econometrica* 86: 85–132.

Egger, Hartmut, and Udo Kreickemeier. 2009. "Firm Heterogeneity and the Labor Market Effects of Trade Liberalization." *International Economic Review* 50: 187–216.

Epifani, Paolo, and Gino Gancia. 2008. "The Skill Bias of World Trade." *Economic Journal* 118: 927–960.

Estevadeordal, Antoni, Brian Frantz, and Alan M. Taylor. 2003. "The Rise and Fall of World Trade: 1870–1939." *Quarterly Journal of Economics* 118: 359–407.

Ethier, Wilfred J. 1982. "National and International Returns to Scale in the Modern Theory of International Trade." *American Economic Review* 72: 389–405.

Fajgelbaum, Pablo D., Gene M. Grossman, and Elhanan Helpman. 2011. "Income Distribution, Product Quality, and International Trade." *Journal of Political Economy* 119: 721–765.

Fajgelbaum, Pablo D., and Amit K. Khandelwal. 2016. "Measuring the Unequal Gains from Trade." *Quarterly Journal of Economics* 131: 1113–1180.

Feenstra, Robert C. 2015. *Advanced International Trade: Theory and Evidence*, Second Edition (Princeton: Princeton University Press).

Feenstra, Robert C., and Gordon H. Hanson. 1996. "Foreign Investment, Outsourcing and Relative Wages." In Robert C. Feenstra, Gene M. Grossman, and Douglas A. Irwin (eds.), *The Political Economy of Trade Policy: Papers in Honor of Jagdish Bhagwati* (Cambridge, MA: The MIT Press).

———. 1997. "Foreign Direct Investment and Relative Wages: Evidence from Mexico's Maquiladoras." *Journal of International Economics* 42: 371–393.

———. 1999. "Productivity Measurement and the Impact of Trade and Technology on Wages: Estimates for the U.S., 1972–1990." *Quarterly Journal of Economics* 114: 907–940.

Ferrie, Joseph P., and Timothy J. Hatton. 2015. "Two Centuries of International Migration." In Barry R. Chiswick and Paul W. Miller (eds.), *Handbook of the Economics of International Migration* Vol. 1A (Amsterdam: North Holland).

Findlay, Ronald, and Kevin H. O'Rourke. 2007. *Power and Plenty: Trade, War, and the World Economy in the Second Millennium* (Princeton: Princeton University Press).

Furceri, Davide, and Prakash Loungani. 2015. "Capital Account Liberalization and Inequality." International Monetary Fund Working Paper WP/15/243.

Goldin, Claudia, and Lawrence F. Katz. 2008. *The Race between Education and Technology* (Cambridge, MA: The Belknap Press of Harvard University Press).

Goldstein, Amy. 2017. *Janesville: An American Story* (New York: Simon and Schuster).

Goos, Maarten, Alan Manning, and Anna Salomons. 2009. "Job Polarization in Europe." *American Economic Review* 99: 58–63.

Grossman, Gene M. 2013. "Heterogeneous Workers and International Trade." *Review of World Economics* 149: 211–245.

Grossman, Gene M., and Elhanan Helpman. 1991a. "Quality Ladders in the Theory of Growth." *Review of Economic Studies* LIIX: 43–61.

———. 1991b. *Innovation and Growth in the Global Economy* (Cambridge, MA: The MIT Press).

———. 2018. "Growth, Trade, and Inequality." *Econometrica* 86: 37–83.

Grossman, Gene M., Elhanan Helpman, and Philipp Kircher. 2017. "Matching, Sorting, and the Distributional Effects of International Trade." *Journal of Political Economy* 125: 224–263.

Grossman, Gene M., and Giovanni Maggi. 2000. "Diversity and Trade." *American Economic Review* 90: 1255–1275.

Grossman, Gene M., and Esteban Rossi-Hansberg. 2008. "Trading Tasks: A Simple Theory of Offshoring." *American Economic Review* 98: 1978–1997.

Hakobyan, Shushanik, and John McLaren. 2016. "Looking for Local Labor Market Effects of NAFTA." *Review of Economics and Statistics* 98: 728–741.

Hanson, Gordon H. 2007. "Globalization, Labor Income, and Poverty in Mexico." In Ann Harrison (ed.), *Globalization and Poverty* (Chicago: The University of Chicago Press).

Harrigan, James, and Ariel Reshef. 2015. "Skill-Biased Heterogeneous Firms, Trade Liberalization and the Skill Premium." *Canadian Journal of Economics* 48: 1024–1066.

Heckscher, Eli F. 1919. "The Effect of Foreign Trade on the Distribution of Income." In Harry Flam and M. June Flanders (eds.), 2001, *Heckscher-Ohlin Trade Theory* (Cambridge, MA: The Massachusetts Institute of Technology Press).

Helpman, Elhanan. 1981. "International Trade in the Presence of Product Differentiation, Economies of Scale and Monopolistic Competition: A Chamberlin-Heckscher-Ohlin Approach." *Journal of International Economics* 11: 305–340.

———— (ed.). 1998. *General Purpose Technologies and Economic Growth* (Cambridge, MA: The Massachusetts Institute of Technology Press).

————. 2004. *The Mystery of Economic Growth* (Cambridge, MA: The Belknap Press of Harvard University Press).

————. 2006. "Trade, FDI, and the Organization of Firms." *Journal of Economic Literature* XLIV: 589–630.

————. 2011. *Understanding Global Trade* (Cambridge, MA: The Belknap Press of Harvard University Press).

————. 2017. "Globalisation and Wage Inequality." *Journal of the British Academy* 5:125–162.

Helpman, Elhanan, Oleg Itskhoki, and Stephen J. Redding. 2010. "Inequality and Unemployment in a Global Economy." *Econometrica* 78: 1239–1283.

Helpman, Elhanan, Oleg Itskhoki, Marc-Andreas Muendler, and Stephen J. Redding. 2017. "Trade and Inequality: From Theory to Estimation." *Review of Economic Studies* 84: 357–405.

Helpman, Elhanan, and Paul R. Krugman. 1985. *Market Structure and Foreign Trade* (Cambridge, MA: The Massachusetts Institute of Technology Press).

Hicks, John R. 1932. *The Theory of Wages* (London: Macmillan and Co., Ltd.).

Houthakker, Hendrik. 1955. "The Pareto Distribution and the Cobb-Douglas Production Function in Activity Analysis." *Review of Economic Studies* 23: 27–31.

Hsieh, Chang-Tai, and Ralph Ossa. 2016. "A Global View of Productivity Growth in China." *Journal of International Economics* 102: 209–224.

Jaumotte, Florence, Subir Lall, and Chris Papageorgiou. 2008. "Rising Income Inequality: Technology, or Trade and Financial Globalization?" International Monetary Fund Working Paper WP/08/185.

Johnson, Robert C., and Guillermo Noguera. 2017. "A Portrait of Trade in Value Added over Four Decades." *Review of Economics and Statistics* 99(5).

Jones, Ronald W. 1965. "The Structure of Simple General Equilibrium Models." *Journal of Political Economy* 73: 557–572.

———. 1971. "A Three-Factor Model in Theory, Trade and History." In Jagdish N. Bhagwati, Ronald W. Jones, Robert A. Mundell, and Jaroslav Vanek (eds.), *Trade, Balance of Payments and Growth: Papers in International Economics in Honor of Charles P. Kindleberger* (Amsterdam: North-Holland): 3–21.

Jones, Ronald W., and Jose A. Scheinkman. 1977. "The Relevance of the Two-Sector Production Model in Trade Theory." *Journal of Political Economy* 85: 909–935.

Katz, Lawrence F., and David H. Autor. 1999. "Changes in the Wage Structure and Earnings Inequality." In Orly Ashenfelter and David Card (eds.), *Handbook of Labor Economics*, Vol. 3 (Amsterdam: North-Holland).

Katz, Lawrence F., and Kevin M. Murphy. 1992. "Changes in Relative Wages, 1963–1987: Supply and Demand Factors." *Quarterly Journal of Economics* 107: 35–78.

Kletzer, Lori G. 2001. *Job Loss from Imports: Measuring the Costs* (Washington, DC: Institute for International Economics).

Kopczuk, Wojciech, Emmanuel Saez, and Jae Song. 2010. "Earnings Inequality and Mobility in the United States: Evidence from Social Security Data Since 1937." *Quarterly Journal of Economics* 125: 91–128.

Kovak, Brian K. 2013. "Regional Effects of Trade Reform: What Is the Correct Measure of Liberalization?" *American Economic Review* 103: 1960–1976.

Kremer, Michael, and Eric Maskin. 1996. "Wage Inequality and Segregation by Skill." National Bureau of Economic Research Working Paper 5718.

Krugman, Paul R. 1979. "Increasing Returns, Monopolistic Competition, and International Trade." *Journal of International Economics* 9: 469–479.

———. 1995. "Growing World Trade: Causes and Consequences." *Brookings Papers on Economic Activity* 1: 327–362.

———. 2000. "Technology, Trade and Factor Prices." *Journal of International Economics* 50: 51–72.

———. 2008. "Trade and Wages, Reconsidered." *Brookings Papers on Economic Activity* 2: 103–138.

Krusell, Per, Lee E. Ohanian, José-Victor Ríos-Rull, and Giovanni L. Violante. 2000. "Capital-Skill Complementarity and Inequality: A Macroeconomic Analysis." *Econometrica* 68: 1029–1053.

Lagakos, David, and Michael E. Waugh. 2013. "Selection, Agriculture, and Cross-Country Productivity Differences." *American Economic Review* 103: 948–980.

Lancaster, Kelvin. 1979. *Variety, Equity, and Efficiency* (New York: Columbia University Press).

Lawrence, Robert, and Matthew J. Slaughter. 1993. "International Trade and American Wages in the 1980s: Giant Sucking Sound or Small Hiccup?" *Brookings Papers on Economic Activity* 1: 161–211.

Lazear, Edward P., and James R. Spletzer. 2012. "Hiring, Churn, and Business Cycles." *American Economic Review* (Papers and Proceedings) 102: 575–579.

Leamer, Edward E. 1998. "In Search of Stolper-Samuelson Linkages between International Trade and Lower Wages." In Susan M. Collins (ed.), *Imports, Exports, and the American Worker* (Washington, DC: Brookings Institution Press).

———. 2000. "What's the Use of Factor Content?" *Journal of International Economics* 50: 17–50.

Lee, Eunhee. 2017. "Trade, Inequality, and the Endogenous Sorting of Heterogeneous Workers." Mimeo, April 22, 2017 version.

Lemieux, Thomas. 2006. "Increasing Residual Wage Inequality: Composition Effects, Noisy Data or Rising Skill Returns?" *American Economic Review* 96: 461–498.

Leontief, Wassily. 1953. "Domestic Production and Foreign Trade: The American Capital Position Re-Examined." *Proceedings of the American Philosophical Society* 97: 332–349.

McCormick, Michael. 2001. *Origins of the European Economy: Communications and Commerce, AD 300–900* (New York: Cambridge University Press).

Machin, Stephen, and John van Reenen. 1998. "Technology and Changes in Skill Structure: Evidence from Seven OECD Countries." *Quarterly Journal of Economics* 113: 1215–1244.

Maddison, Angus. 1995. *Monitoring the World Economy* (Paris: Organization for Economic Cooperation and Development).

———. 2001. *The World Economy: A Millennial Perspective* (Paris: Organization for Economic Cooperation and Development).

Maskin, Eric. 2015. "Why Haven't Global Markets Reduced Inequality in Emerging Economies?" *World Bank Economic Review* 29 (Supplement): S48–S52.

Melitz, Marc J. 2003. "The Impact of Trade on Intra-Industry Reallocations and Aggregate Industry Productivity." *Econometrica* 71: 1695–1725.

Melitz, Marc J., and Stephen J. Redding. 2014. "Heterogeneous Firms and Trade." In Gita Gopinath, Elhanan Helpman, and Kenneth Rogoff (eds.), *Handbook of International Economics* (Amsterdam: North Holland).

Melitz, Marc J., and Daniel Trefler. 2012. "Gains from Trade when Firms Matter." *Journal of Economic Perspectives* 26: 91–118.

Milanovic, Branko. 2016. *Global Inequality: A New Approach for the Age of Globalization* (Cambridge, MA: The Belknap Press of Harvard University Press).

Mincer, Jacob. 1974. *Schooling, Experience, and Earnings* (New York: Columbia University Press).

Morelli, Salvatore, Timothy Smeeding, and Jeffrey Thompson. 2015. "Post-1970 Trends in Within-Country Inequality and Poverty: Rich and Middle-Income Countries." Chapter 8 in Anthony B. Atkinson, and

Francois Bourguignon (eds.), *Handbook of Income Distribution*, Vol. 2A (Amsterdam: North–Holland).

Morrisson, Christian, and Fabrice Murtin. 2011. "Internal Income Inequality and Global Inequality." Working Paper 26, Development Policies, Fondation pour les Études et Recherchés sur le Développement International.

Mortensen, Dale T., and Christopher A. Pissarides. 1994. "Job Creation and Job Destruction in the Theory of Unemployment." *Review of Economic Studies* 61: 397–415.

Oberfield, Ezra, and Devesh Raval. 2014. "Micro Data and Macro Technology." National Bureau of Economic Research Working Paper 20452.

Ohnsorge, Franziska, and Daniel Trefler. 2007. "Sorting It Out: International Trade with Heterogeneous Workers." *Journal of Political Economy* 115: 868–892.

OECD. 2015. *In It Together: Why Less Inequality Benefits All* (Paris: OECD Publishing).

Ohlin, Bertil. 1924. "The Theory of Trade." In Harry Flam and M. June Flanders (eds.), 2001, *Heckscher-Ohlin Trade Theory* (Cambridge, MA: The Massachusetts Institute of Technology Press).

———. 1933. *Interregional and International Trade* (Cambridge, MA: Harvard University Press).

Oi, Walter Y., and T. L. Idson. 1999. "Firm Size and Wages." In Orly Ashenfelter and David Card (eds.), *Handbook of Labor Economics*, Vol. 3 (Amsterdam: Elsevier).

Pavcnik, Nina. 2017. "The Impact of Trade on Inequality in Developing Countries." National Bureau of Economic Research Working Paper 23878.

Peri, Giovanni. 2016. "Immigrants, Productivity, and Labor Markets." *Journal of Economic Perspectives* 30 (4): 3–30.

Pierce, Justin R., and Peter K. Schott. 2016. "The Surprisingly Swift Decline of US Manufacturing Employment." *American Economic Review* 106: 1632–1662.

Piketty, Thomas. 2014. *Capital in the Twenty-First Century*, trans. Arthur Goldhammer (Cambridge, MA: The Belknap Press of Harvard University Press).

Piketty, Thomas, Emmanuel Saez, and Gabriel Zucman. 2018. "Distributional National Accounts: Methods and Estimates for the United States." *Quarterly Journal of Economics* 133: 553–609.

Razin, Assaf, and Efraim Sadka. 2014. *Migration States and Welfare States: Why Is America Different from Europe?* (New York: Palgrave Macmillan).

Rodrik, Dani. 2015. *Economics Rules: The Rights and Wrongs of the Dismal Science* (New York: W. W. Norton & Company).

Romalis, John. 2007. "NAFTA's and CUSFTA's Impact on International Trade." *Review of Economics and Statistics* 89: 416–435.

Romer, Paul M. 1990. "Endogenous Technological Change." *Journal of Political Economy* 98: S71–S102.

Sachs, Jeffrey D., and Howard Shatz. 1994. "Trade and Jobs in U.S. Manufacturing." *Brookings Papers on Economic Activity* 2: 1–84.

Sampson, Thomas. 2014. "Selection into Trade and Wage Inequality." *American Economic Journal: Microeconomics* 6: 157–202.

Scheidel, Walter. 2017. *The Great Leveler: Violence and the History of Inequality from the Stone Age to the Twenty-First Century* (Princeton: Princeton University Press).

Spence, Michael E. 1976. "Product Selection, Fixed Costs, and Monopolistic Competition." *Review of Economic Studies* 43: 217–236.

Stolper, Wolfgang W., and Paul A. Samuelson. 1941. "Protection and Real Wages." *Review of Economic Studies* IX: 58–73.

Topalova, Petia. 2007. "Trade Liberalization, Poverty, and Inequality: Evidence from Indian Districts." In Ann Harrison (ed.), *Globalization and Poverty* (Chicago: The University of Chicago Press).

———. 2010. "Factor Immobility and Regional Impacts of Trade Liberalization: Evidence on Poverty from India." *American Economic Journal: Applied Economics* 2: 1–41.

Trefler, Daniel. 1995. "The Case of the Missing Trade and Other Mysteries." *American Economic Review* 85: 1029–1046.

———. 2004. "The Long and Short of the Canada-U.S. Free Trade Agreement." *American Economic Review* 94: 870–895.

Trefler, Daniel, and Susan Chun Zhu. 2010. "The Structure of Factor Content Predictions." *Journal of International Economics* 82: 195–207.

Vanek, Jaroslav. 1968. "The Factor Proportions Theory: The N-Factor Case." *Kyklos* 21: 749–754.

Van Zanden, Jan Luiten, Joerg Baten, Peter Foldvari, and Bas van Leeuwen. 2014. "The Changing Shape of Global Inequality 1820–2000: Exploring a New Dataset." *The Review of Income and Wealth* 60: 279–297.

Verhoogen, Eric. 2008. "Trade, Quality Upgrading, and Wage Inequality in the Mexican Manufacturing Sector: Theory and Evidence from an Exchange Rate Shock." *Quarterly Journal of Economics* 123: 489–530.

Wood, Adrian. 1994. *North-South Trade, Employment and Inequality: Changing Fortunes in a Skill-Driven World* (Oxford: Clarendon Press).

World Trade Organization. 2016. *World Trade Statistical Review 2016* (Geneva).

Wright, Greg C. 2014. "Revisiting the Employment Impact of Offshoring." *European Economic Review* 66: 63–83.

Xu, Bin. 2001. "Factor Bias, Sector Bias, and the Effects of Technical Progress on Relative Factor Prices." *Journal of International Economics* 54: 2–25.

Yeaple, Stephen R. 2005. "A Simple Model of Firm Heterogeneity, International Trade, and Wages." *Journal of International Economics* 65: 1–20.

Zhu, Susan Chun, and Daniel Trefler. 2005. "Trade and Inequality in Developing Countries: A General Equilibrium Analysis." *Journal of International Economics* 65: 21–48.

Index